DAIRY FREE
RECIPES&PREPARATION

Angela Litzinger is an expert in dairy- and gluten-free recipe development and living. When not puttering around the kitchen, hanging out with her husband and three kids (or the flock of sassy chickens in the back yard), she teaches food preservation and allergen-free cooking classes, contributes articles and recipes to numerous publications, and speaks to local and national organizations about the dairy- and gluten-free diet and other important allergy issues. Angela documents her family's allergen-free journey on angelaskitchen.com.

Publisher & Creative Director: Nick Wells
Senior Project Editor: Catherine Taylor
Copy Editor: Kathy Steer
Art Director: Mike Spender
Layout Design: Jane Ashley
Digital Design & Production: Chris Herbert
Proofreader: Dawn Laker

Special thanks to Angelica Stevenson, Natalia Camicia, Frances Bodiam.

FLAME TREE PUBLISHING
6 Melbray Mews, Fulham,
London SW6 3NS, United Kingdom
www.flametreepublishing.com

This edition published 2019

Images: © StockFood and the following: 47l Castilho, Rua; 63 Gräfe & Unzer Verlag / Zanin, Melanie; 66 Hussey, Clinton; 71 Lawton, Becky; 75 Weymann, Frank; 85 Gräfe & Unzer Verlag / Lang, Coco; 143 Laniak, Malgorzata; 181 Janssen, Valerie; 209 Wischnewski, Jan; 210 Indycka, Dorota. Courtesy of Shutterstock.com and © the following: 3 & 221 Anna Kurzaeva; 6r Alexander Raths; 6l Kristi Blokhin; 7l, 79, 168 Oksana Mizina; 7r Rawpixel.com; 13t margouillat photo; 13b, 30 Yulia Furman; 14 Sementsova Lesia; 17bl D. Pimborough; 17t espies; 17br evilbeau; 19tr, 33b beats1; 19tl Malivan_Iuliia; 19bl, 45r Sea Wave; 19br Sunny Forest; 20t, 42t, 69 & back cover tl, 187 Alexander Prokopenko; 20b Krasula; 23t Andrey_Popov; 23b Malykalexa; 25t Anastasiia Malinich; 25bl barmalini; 25br KieferPix; 27bl MaraZe; 27br Noam Armonn; 27tr Roman Diachkin; 27tl zjuzjaka; 28b Antonio Guillem; 28t Stock-Asso; 33t sheff; 34r Jat306; 34l Sergey Ryzhov; 35 Antonina Vlasova; 37b El Nariz; 37t Goksi; 38, 42b marilyn barbone; 41r Igor Palamarchuk; 41l Malyugin; 41t Timolina; 45t baibaz; 45l iprachenko; 46r, 98 Africa Studio; 46l Luis Echeverri Urrea; 47r peterzsuzsa; 49t Dalaifood; 49r Makistock; 49l Mohiniraj Bhave; 50t Gaf_Lila; 50bl Mike_shots; 50br photopixel; 52bl Dmitry_Evs; 52br sdrug07; 53br Luna Vandoorne; 53bl Yuliia Kononenko; 55 zarzamora; 58 Lucky_elephant; 65 DronG; 72 Ksenija Toyechkina; 77, 100, 128, 194 Liliya Kandrashevich; 80 Justyna Pankowska; 83 Danie Nel Photography; 87 viennetta; 91 AS Food studio; 93 Fascinadora; 94 HealthyLauraCom; 97 zoryanchik; 103 vanillaechoes; 105, 106, 116 Elena Veselova; 109 kiboka; 113 MasterQ; 115 & back cover tr oxyzay; 118, 182 Lisovskaya Natalia; 121 Natasha Breen; 122 Melica; 127 & 224 Olga Gorchichko; 131, 135, 213 Brent Hofacker; 133, 215 Anna_Pustynnikova; 136 Teri Virbickis; 138 olepeshkina; 145, 216 Nataliia Harahliad; 149 vm2002; 151 & back cover bl SherSor; 152 Vania Georgieva; 157, 175 & back cover br Elena Shashkina; 159 SergeBertasiusPhotography; 160 casanisa; 162 AnjelikaGr; 165 Stephanie Frey; 167 Josie Grant; 171 Bartosz Luczak; 177 BEATA PAWLAK; 179 Magdanatka; 188 pearl7; 191, 202 & front cover Tatiana Vorona; 193 VICUSCHKA; 199 Lynne Ann Mitchell; 207 Elisabeth Coelfen; 219 AnikonaAnn.

DAIRY FREE
RECIPES&PREPARATION

Angela Litzinger

FLAME TREE
PUBLISHING

CONTENTS

INTRODUCTION

On the first date with my husband, we both found out we had a shared passion for frozen yogurt. On subsequent dates, we would look for new tastes to enjoy, exploring flavour combinations and surprising each other with new brands we found at the market. Even after all these years, we still look back fondly on a particularly tasty apple-granola frozen yogurt combo. The two of us plus frozen yogurt seemed like a match made in heaven.

DIAGNOSIS

However, shortly after we married, I started getting sick, and continued to have various symptoms, increasing in severity. After several months, and several trips to various doctors, I was finally diagnosed with a dairy allergy. What was a dairy-loving girl to do?

RESEARCH

My answer was to get in the kitchen and start experimenting. I pored over vegan cookbooks at the library, bought all kinds of mysterious ingredients at the local supermarket and played around with various seasonings. There wasn't a lot of information or recipes back in the early 1990s if you wanted to make anything homemade that seemed even remotely cheesy, and forget about any dairy-free products at the supermarket (if you could find them) that weren't soy based.

REVELATION

After lots of trial and error, I was able to recreate the flavours and textures we missed in our food. After having children, it became even more important to me to perfect versions of my grandmother's special occasion recipes so those food traditions could

be carried on. After all, Christmas just didn't seem the same without eggnog or rice pudding, so I needed to find a way to make them dairy free and still delicious enough to make Grandma proud.

LEARNING TO LIVE WITHOUT DAIRY (AND GLUTEN!)

For those of you who are curious, my dairy allergy specifically consists of a severe allergy to both the proteins casein and whey in milk, and now I carry an EpiPen. My mum said I had a dairy allergy as a baby, but little did we know that I did not outgrow it, leading to years of health issues, including migraines starting at the age of 10 and persistent ear infections throughout my childhood and adult years, including one that caused my ear drum to rupture a month before my wedding. Later in life, I was also diagnosed with coeliac disease, so my diet now is a one-two punch of gluten- and dairy-free deliciousness.

Do I miss all the dairy-filled foods out there? I can honestly say that with all the other wonderful foods and cultural cuisines to explore, I would be hard pressed to ever get tired of a dairy-free diet. My hope is that in this book you will find new recipes to try and a few family favourites that you can come to rely on.

WHAT YOU NEED TO KNOW

WHAT IS A DAIRY-FREE DIET?

A dairy-free diet is one that omits milk (from any animal) and all related products, such as yogurt, butter, ice cream, puddings and cheese. This also includes the by-products of dairy that is broken down from milk for food manufacturing purposes, such as milk fat, lactose, whey and casein. A dairy-free diet does not, therefore, include eliminating eggs and egg products (*see* page 21).

People who are lactose intolerant may choose to only reduce or eliminate foods that contain lactose, and not all dairy products. Some people with dairy intolerance may be able to have smaller amounts of foods containing milk proteins, or find that fermented dairy products are easier on their digestive systems. Some people sensitive to cow's milk may even find that products made with milk from other animals, such as goats, can be tolerated better by their system. People with a milk food allergy, on the other hand, must completely eliminate all milk proteins from their diets and find alternatives.

LABELS CAN BE CONFUSING

Some terminology can be confusing when trying to understand what is dairy free.

'Vegan' Product Labels

Products labelled as 'vegan' mean they have been made without any animal products or by-products, such as dairy, eggs, gelatine and honey. Products labelled as 'vegan' should always be dairy free by ingredients, however, always check ingredient labels as mistakes can happen. For people with severe dairy allergies, check with the manufacturer, as cross-contamination could be a risk, depending on how the product was processed.

'Kosher' Product Labels

Products labelled as 'kosher' are foods that meet Jewish dietary laws. These dietary laws prohibit the consumption of certain foods and mean some foods must be prepared in certain ways. For those with food allergies, the most important thing to know is that the dietary law prohibits the mixing of meat products and dairy products, with products marked accordingly. However, a dairy-allergic person cannot rely on the 'kosher pareve' designation or the lack of a kosher dairy label to know if a particular food is safe. This is because it is possible for a food to contain a trace level of dairy contamination, which might be a problem for someone with a severe allergy, and still be considered 'kosher dairy free' from the standpoint of Jewish dietary laws. It is possible that traces of allergens may be in kosher foods, just like any other manufactured food. Read the ingredient statement on every item purchased and contact the manufacturer to determine if a product is safe for your needs.

'Non-dairy' Product Labels

Be very cautious of the term 'non-dairy'. Non-dairy products may or may not be free of milk-based ingredients. In the United States, the regulatory definition actually allows the presence of the milk protein casein (also called caseinate) in products labelled 'non-dairy'. 'Non-dairy' is commonly used as a label on coffee creamers made with caseinate rather than milk or cream. However, the term 'caseinate' will appear in the ingredient statement and must be followed by an explanation, such as 'a milk derivative'. 'Non-dairy' is also used on other products containing caseinates, such as soy-based cheeses and whipped toppings. Once again, carefully check the ingredient list, making sure the product does not contain any unsafe ingredients when following a dairy-free diet.

'Dairy-free' Product Labels

'Dairy free' should mean the product is free of dairy, but, depending on the country, this may only mean it is free of cow dairy, and does not apply to other animal milks, such as sheep, goat or buffalo. For those with a very severe dairy allergy or intolerance, even trace amounts of milk proteins may cause a reaction, even from milk from other animal sources. In product manufacturing, 'dairy-free' products may again be cross-contaminated with trace amounts of dairy due to the use of shared equipment during manufacturing.

Read all food labels to ensure you are truly getting a product that is free of all dairy products. For sufferers of a severe allergy or intolerance, always consider cross-contamination potential. Contact directly the manufacturers of any product purchased that may pose a cross-contamination risk to verify product safety before consuming.

DAIRY FOODS TO AVOID

There are many dairy-based foods and ingredients to avoid when eating dairy free:

Butter (including butter fat, butter oil, and may also include some brands of margarine)

Buttermilk

Casein

Caseinates (such as calcium caseinate, potassium caseinate, sodium caseinate, magnesium caseinate and ammonium caseinate)

Cheese

Cheese spreads

Cream

Cottage and ricotta cheese

Curds

Custards and puddings

Evaporated and condensed milk

Fromage frais

Ghee

Hydrolysed casein/whey

Hydrolysates

Ice cream ('gelato'), ice milk and sherbet

Kefir

Lactalbumin

Lactoglobulin

Lactose

Lactulose

Malted milk

Milk (in any form, including reduced lactose milk)

Milk fat

Milk powder

Milk solids

Clockwise from top: ghee is clarified butter, malted milk is still milk, and classic custard is mostly pure dairy

Non-fat dry milk powder

Rennet casein

Skimmed milk powder

Sour cream

Whey

Whey solids, whey protein and whey
 sugar

Yogurt

OTHER FOODS THAT MAY CONTAIN DAIRY

Dairy elements can often be found in other ready-made foods, such as the following, some of which may surprise you:

Artificial or so-called 'dairy-free' cream

Batters, everything from waffles and
 pancakes to ones for deep-frying

Biscuits and cookies

Breads and other baked goods

Caramel

Chocolate and chocolate products

Crème pâtissière (pastry cream/
 custard)

Creamed vegetables

Deli meats

Dips

Frozen shop-bought meals

Hot chocolate and instant latte mixes

Icing and frostings

Many margarines

Nougat

Pre-made mashed potatoes and
 instant potato mixes

Rice pudding and other baked
 puddings

Sauces

Scones

Smoothies, often made with milk and/
 or yogurt

Some animal fats

Some sweeteners

White sauce

Clockwise from top left: whey is the liquid by-product of cheese-making; deli meats may contain lactose, casein or caseinates, added as emulsifiers or flavour enhancers; fruit smoothies may also contain milk or yogurt; and ready-made or powdered mashed potato mix may contain dairy

WHAT ABOUT EGGS?

Although we know eggs come from chickens, there is often confusion whether eggs are considered a dairy product. Perhaps this is because eggs are often found in the dairy section of the supermarket and are often grouped with milk products on nutritional posters.

A dairy product is any product of the mammary glands of mammals such as cows, goats, buffalo, sheep and the products made from them, such as milk, butter, cheese and cream. People who need to avoid dairy because of milk allergies or are lactose intolerant, and do not have an allergy or intolerance to eggs, can consume eggs as part of their diet.

Besides allergies, there are some people who do eliminate both dairy and eggs from their diet. Vegans are people who choose to abstain from all animal products and by-products, meaning not only do they not eat meat and fish, but also dairy, eggs, honey and all manner of products derived in some way from animals.

There are also some Jewish communities that do not consume eggs with dairy if the egg was found inside the chicken and not laid. An unlaid egg is considered meat and it is not kosher to consume meat and dairy together. This is not because eggs that have been laid are considered dairy, but only that ones that were not laid are considered meat.

WHY GO DAIRY FREE?

People follow a dairy-free diet for a variety of reasons. Some are allergic to the proteins in milk, while others lack the enzyme lactase, which digests the sugar in milk, called lactose. Others avoid milk out of compassion towards animals that produce milk, or follow dietary laws, while others are searching for relief from digestive issues, skin problems or respiratory issues.

LACTOSE INTOLERANCE

People with lactose intolerance are unable to fully digest the sugar, or lactose, in milk. As a result, symptoms such as bloating, gas, nausea, abdominal cramps and diarrhoea can occur after eating or drinking dairy products. A deficiency of the enzyme lactase is usually responsible for lactose intolerance. It has been estimated that 70 per cent of the world's population has some degree of lactose intolerance. After weaning, people no longer need the ability to digest their mother's milk, so they naturally begin producing less lactase over time.

COW'S MILK PROTEIN INTOLERANCE

Cow's Milk Protein Intolerance (CMPI) is an abnormal reaction by the body's immune system to protein in cow's milk, usually diagnosed in infants. The reaction can cause damage to the stomach and intestinal tract. Symptoms of lethargy, fevers, hives, eczema, severe diarrhoea or vomiting, weight loss, and blood in the stools usually develop within the first week of starting cow's milk in the child's diet. Infants diagnosed with CMPI will need to be on a cow's milk-free formula or breast fed by a mother on a cow's milk-free diet for 6–12 months before re-introducing cow's milk back to the diet. Fortunately, CMPI resolves in 50 per cent of children by the time they are one year old and 90 per cent of children by the age of six.

ALLERGIES

A milk allergy differs from lactose intolerance. Milk allergy is an overreaction of the immune system to specific proteins found in dairy. There is no tolerating even a lactose-free option if someone wants to avoid hives, rash, trouble breathing or even anaphylaxis. A milk allergy reaction can be severe and life-threatening. Dairy ranks in the top eight food allergens in the United States, the top 11 in Canada and the top 14 in the UK. Cow's milk is the usual cause of milk allergy, but milk from sheep, buffalo, goats and other mammals can also cause a reaction.

GALACTOSEMIA

Galactosemia is a rare genetic metabolic disorder. A person diagnosed with galactosemia must inherit a gene for galactosemia from both their mother and their father. A person with galactosemia does not produce the enzyme needed to process galactose, which the body breaks down from lactose from foods such as milk and from several fruits, vegetables and other foods. The build-up of galactose in the body is very toxic and as many as 75 per cent of infants with galactosemia will die if the condition is untreated. Serious complications, such as cataracts, brain damage, infection, ovarian failure and liver damage or failure can also occur. Diagnosis of galactosemia is usually made within the first week of life by a heel-prick blood test as part of standard newborn screening. Treatment is a strict removal of all lactose and galactose from the diet.

Even goat's milk and buffalo mozzarella can trigger dairy allergy

VEGAN

A person who follows a vegan diet avoids all animal and animal-derived products for health or environmental reasons or out of compassion for the animals that produce food products commonly eaten by others. Ethically, vegans are usually not only opposed to killing animals for food, but also believe animals have the right to be free from human use as food, clothing, entertainment or for scientific experimentation. A vegan diet not only excludes the meat from any animal or fish, but also eggs, milk and any animal products and by-products, such as honey, gelatine, albumin, whey, casein and some forms of vitamin D3. Vegan foods will generally be safe to eat on a dairy-free diet, but as with all products, double check that cross-contamination with dairy has not occurred.

PALEO

A Paleo (short for 'Paleolithic') diet is an eating plan modelled on what might have been eaten in prehistoric human diets. Other names for a Paleo diet include caveman diet, hunter-gatherer diet and the Stone Age diet. A Paleo diet typically includes foods that during the Paleolithic era could have been obtained by hunting and gathering, such as lean meats, fish, fruits, vegetables, honey, nuts and seeds. A Paleo diet limits foods that only became common after farming became widespread, such as legumes, grains and dairy products. That being said, many people following a Paleo diet, who will not eat cheese and yogurt or drink milk, will still use grass-fed butter and ghee, a clarified butter product. Before eating a dish described as 'Paleo', check the ingredients list and how it was prepared to make sure it is completely free of milk products.

KOSHER

As we have mentioned, the Jewish religion forbids the consumption of certain foods, and foods that have been prepared in certain ways, according to the regulations of

Top: vegan diets exclude all animal-related products
Bottom left: typical 'Paleo' foods do not include dairy

kashrut (dietary law). Those foods that are permitted are termed 'kosher'. Milk can be deemed kosher as long as it comes from kosher animals, but Jewish people may choose to go dairy free in order to simplify life, since a key kosher rule is that milk and meat must be kept separate in all ways, including using separate crockery and utensils for each.

OTHER HEALTH REASONS

Some people try a dairy-free diet to see if it helps them alleviate other heath issues, such as sinus and respiratory issues, reflux, stomach cramps and aches, skin issues (such as eczema, psoriasis or acne), sluggish digestion, headaches or migraines, fatigue, sleep issues, joint stiffness, difficulty with concentration or 'foggy brain'. If you are wondering if a sensitivity to dairy could be contributing to any health issues, it is best to work with your doctor, allergist, nutritionist or dietitian. They can help set up an elimination diet to see if dairy, another food or a different cause is the culprit. An elimination diet involves removing foods from your diet that you suspect your body does not tolerate well. After a few weeks, when the unwanted symptoms have cleared, the removed foods are re-introduced, one at a time, during which time you watch to see if symptoms return. It is always safest to try an elimination diet under the supervision of a medical professional, as food re-introduction has been known to trigger dangerous reactions in some people.

MAKING THE TRANSITION

While it isn't always easy to adjust to the dairy-free life, there are simple ways to make the transition much easier.

BE PATIENT

It is easy to be overwhelmed by change, and the challenge of eating dairy free can feel like a big step. At first, it might seem like the diet eliminates all the food you love to eat and it could take up to six months to begin to feel comfortable with the diet and confident about your food choices. Be patient as you adjust and don't be too hard on yourself. Don't expect to have it all figured out overnight. It will get easier over time as you learn more.

It is normal to feel grief over having to give up foods you have eaten your whole life. I chose to combat this by taking just one Christmas recipe every year or two from my grandmother and converting it to be dairy free. I did this instead of working on the whole meal all at once. Having just one recipe to focus on converting helped ensure success in the long run, and over time, the whole meal has become made dairy free.

KNOW WHAT TO LOOK FOR

Milk is a confusing and sneaky food. It is hidden on labels under names like casein, caseinate and whey. In the United States, under federal labelling laws, a product can be labelled as 'non-dairy' as long as it contains less than 0.5% milk protein by weight. In the dairy-free community, the terms 'dairy free' and 'non-dairy' are often used interchangeably, but the terms represent very different things on food labels, which can be life-threatening for a person with a dairy allergy or sensitivity. In the UK, there is no similar official allowance for a limited amount of milk protein for 'non-dairy', and anything that claims to be dairy 'free' must not use any ingredients, or 'compound ingredients', such as additives and processing aids, containing dairy. The only exception is that in EU legislation, thresholds for making a 'lactose-free' claim have been defined for infant and follow-on formula, where the rules stipulate that the lactose content should be ≤ 10 mg/100 kcal (2.5 mg/100 kJ). Research what to look for, keeping a list with you as you shop, so you can compare any ingredients you don't recognize with the list of dairy-derived ingredients.

CHOOSE WHOLE FOODS

Remember that just because something is labelled dairy free does not mean it is good for you. When first going dairy free, all the prepared products can be very tempting, however, a doughnut is still a doughnut whether it is dairy free or not. Concentrate at first on eating plain, healthy foods to regain your health. This also ensures that your food has not come into contact with any dairy ingredients during processing. When you are feeling better and your confidence in your dairy-free options is higher, then start to experiment in the kitchen with more ambitious recipes. If a cooking experiment goes awry? Take the time to laugh, enjoy the process and try again.

A healthy nutrient-rich diet without dairy is more than possible, but since we tend to use dairy as a primary nutrient source, make sure your diet contains vitamins D and B12 as well as magnesium, protein and calcium, as you will be missing them due to removing dairy-containing foods. There are plenty of dairy-free alternatives fortified with the same

nutrients found in milk. Several foods can help round out your nutritional needs, such as dark leafy greens, seeds and nuts. For vitamin D, the sun is our best source, so get out and enjoy those sunny days, knowing you are doing your body good. According to a UK study and published in the *Journal of Investigative Dermatology,* healthy levels of vitamin D were maintained with 13 minutes of midday sunlight exposure three times a week during the summer. It is recommended to get 10–30 minutes of midday sunlight several times per week. Your exposure time should be limited, based on how sensitive your skin is to sunlight. However, generally speaking, to be sure not to get sunburn, if you are planning on being in the sun for longer than 20 minutes, you should apply sunscreen 30 minutes before sun exposure. As with any major changes in diet or lifestyle, seek advice from your doctor, a registered nutritionist or dietitian to ensure your diet is balanced and contains all you need to thrive.

BECOME A LABEL READER & SHOP AROUND

While your local market may have all the things you need, check out other grocers, health-food stores, shops and even online to see what they have in stock. Different markets carry different things and the price point can vary greatly.

That being said, be sure to read labels and check it is safe for eating on the dairy-free diet. Remember, a label that says 'dairy free' doesn't always mean it is free of dairy proteins! Companies often change the formula of their products, so it pays to read the label on products every time you buy them.

Don't try to figure out all the products at once. As you start eating dairy free, try to mainly shop the perimeter of the market, choosing whole fruits, vegetables and proteins. Pick out only one or two products to try or to research. Many companies now list their phone numbers on the packet, so you can give them a call on your phone while shopping if you have a question about an ingredient.

Those with a life-threatening allergy or intolerance should avoid processed products that lack nutritional information. When dining out, it is important to let your waiter know about

your allergy, as this information is not as readily available in restaurants as it is in the supermarket. You can often check most menus online ahead of time for an idea of what to get. Specifically, look for allergen and nutritional menus to see the breakdown of ingredients.

PLAN AHEAD

Making a menu plan helps a lot when shopping. Not only can it keep your budget under control, but you won't be tempted to buy things that are not on the list that contain dairy when you know what it is you will be making that week. Freeze leftovers as individual meals for days you are too busy to cook. Keep a stock of dairy-free snacks and other food on hand that are portable for those times when you know you will be away for several hours and unsure of where to safely eat. I like to keep a stash of dairy-free cupcakes in my freezer for impromptu birthday celebrations.

STAY POSITIVE

Concentrate on what you can eat, not on what you can't eat. Remember that most of the nutritious foods you are supposed to eat to stay healthy are naturally dairy free. This includes plain meat, fish, poultry, beans, eggs, vegetables, fruits, rice, nuts, herbs, spices and legumes. When you would like a treat, there are now plenty of choices to choose from when you get a craving for something you haven't learned to make from scratch. Try not to rely on pre-made processed foods for all your meals (you're trying to regain your health, right?), but for the occasional treat, or if you have a particularly busy day, it is nice to know the options are out there.

Milk is just one food, and while it is used in a myriad of applications, remember there are thousands of other foods. Experiment with new seasonings, herbs, nuts and seeds. Try different grains or a fruit or vegetable you haven't had before. Check out recipes from other cultures. There are several cuisines that naturally use very little dairy. Have fun exploring new things.

Most foods are naturally dairy free

DAIRY-FREE STAPLES

Going dairy free can seem like a challenge at first, but a well-stocked cupboard or pantry can make the transition a lot easier. By keeping a few staples on hand at all times, you can create delicious meals that satisfy your dietary needs and your taste buds. I always have the following staple groups in my kitchen.

PROTEIN SOURCES

Such as: eggs; wild fish (salmon, cod, grouper, herring, trout, sardines); shellfish and molluscs (prawns/shrimp, crab, lobster, mussels, clams, oysters), meats (pork, beef, lamb, liver, chicken, turkey, duck, ostrich); wild game, legumes and lentils, nuts (almonds, cashews, peanuts, pecans, walnuts, hazelnuts) and seeds (flaxseed, sunflower seeds, pumpkin seeds, sesame seeds, chia seeds).

VEGETABLES

Such as: leafy greens and lettuces, spring greens (collards), (bell) peppers, cucumber, tomato, courgettes (zucchini), squash, pumpkin, aubergines (eggplant), spinach, broccoli, kale, chard, cabbage, carrots, onions, mushrooms, cauliflower, Brussels sprouts, sauerkraut, artichoke, alfalfa sprouts, green beans, celery, pak choi/bok choy, radishes, watercress, turnip, asparagus, garlic, leek, fennel, shallots, potatoes, sweet potatoes, spring onions (scallions), ginger.

FRUITS

Such as: strawberries, blueberries, grapes, cranberries, figs, dates, nectarines, blackberries, apples, apricots, cherries, bananas, plums, peaches, lemons, mangoes, melons, limes, oranges and clementines.

WHOLE GRAINS

Such as: brown rice, quinoa, sorghum, wild rice, amaranth, teff, buckwheat, millet and oats.

HEALTHY FATS

Such as: extra virgin olive oil, coconut oil, avocado oil, flaxseed oil and sesame oil. It can also include avocados, olives, coconuts and nut and seed butters. Raw nuts are purchased whenever on sale to be on hand for dairy-free cheeses and sauces.

HERBS, SEASONINGS & CONDIMENTS

Such as: salt, black pepper, allspice, nutmeg, onion powder, cinnamon, dried ginger, cloves, Italian seasoning, garlic powder, basil, chilli powder, caraway seeds, etc. Just be sure to read labels to make sure you are getting herb and spice blends that are dairy free and do not contain natural butter flavourings, dried milk powders or casein. Depending on what country you live in or what brand you buy, ketchups, mustard, chutney, BBQ sauce, mayonnaise, tartare sauce, taco sauce and Worcestershire sauce may not contain dairy. Prepared horseradish, pesto, dressings and dips will need to be checked for dairy ingredients.

BAKING INGREDIENTS

Baking powder, bicarbonate of soda (baking soda), baking yeast, cream of tartar, sugar, brown sugar, honey, molasses, maple syrup, icing (confectioners') sugar, pure vanilla and almond extract, cocoa powder, chocolate chips (be sure they are dairy free).

Flours

Such as: wheat flour, plain (all-purpose) flour, and gluten-free flours such as brown rice, bean, cornmeal, buckwheat, millet, quinoa, sorghum, teff, nut and amaranth flours.

Starches, Binders & Gums

OAT FLOUR

Milled from oats, oat flour is a great source of dietary fibre, and can also add body to a dairy-free smoothie or sauce.

CHESTNUT, ALMOND & OTHER NUT FLOURS

High in protein. Used in small amounts in recipes, finely ground nut flours enhance the taste of many baked goods and can improve the rise. A great substitute for non-fat dry milk powder in recipes.

SWEET RICE FLOUR

Milled from 'sticky' or 'glutinous' rice, a very starchy rice with great binding properties. Much higher in starch than other rice flours. When added to dairy-free cheese sauces, it creates a nice stretchy texture.

POTATO STARCH

Starch from potatoes, a great replacement for cornflour (cornstarch).

TAPIOCA FLOUR (STARCH)

Made from the root of the cassava plant. Tapioca flour helps bind recipes and improves the texture of baked goods. Tapioca helps add a fantastic stretchy texture to dairy-free cheese recipes when they are melted.

CORNFLOUR (CORNSTARCH)

Made from the endosperm of corn. Used to thicken sauces and add tenderness to dairy-free baked goods.

ARROWROOT

Made from the roots of the arrowroot plant. It can be used as a direct substitute for cornflour.

POWDERED GELATINE

This is an odourless, tasteless and colourless thickening agent, commonly made from beef, pork or fish. It must be allowed to soak in water for 5 minutes, or to 'bloom',

ensuring that the gelatine dissolves evenly in a mixture. Helps to stabilize and give the correct texture to some dairy-free cheeses and recipes.

AGAR AGAR

One of the most common vegetarian alternatives to gelatine. Made from a seaweed, it comes in powdered or flaked form. When replacing gelatine, a one-to-one ratio of powdered agar will give best results.

PSYLLIUM

Psyllium husks are from the seeds of a plant that is high in dietary fibre and used as a food thickener, emulsifier and binder. Psyllium works well in dairy-free cheeses by keeping them a 'gooey' texture when they are heated.

LECITHIN

This is essential for creating an emulsion, allowing liquids and oils to mix and stay mixed without separating. Commonly made from soy or sunflower, lecithin is available

Above left to right: powdered gelatine, psyllium

in liquid or granular form. Granular lecithin must be refrigerated and smell fresh, not rancid. Liquid lecithin does not need refrigeration.

XANTHAN GUM

Produced by the fermentation of sugars, xanthan gum adds volume and stretch to baked goods and is used as an emulsifier and binder in dressing and sauces.

GUAR GUM

This is a white flour-like substance made from an East Indian seed, used as a binder, like xanthan gum. The two can be used interchangeably.

OTHER ITEMS TO KEEP ON HAND

- Non-dairy beverages (such as almond or coconut milk)
- Tea and coffee
- Canned coconut milk and coconut cream
- Canned pumpkin
- Unsweetened apple purée (applesauce)
- Pre-made pasta
- Spaghetti sauce, diced tomatoes, chopped tomatoes
- Corn tortillas
- Dried fruit

Top: granular lecithin; bottom left: the guar or cluster bean plant,
the seeds of which are used to manufacture guar gum

TOOLS & TECHNIQUES

When you go dairy free, you inevitably will spend some time in the kitchen, so it is a good idea to get a few tools to help you cook some great meals.

A WORD ABOUT CROSS-CONTAMINATION

Be sure to explain what is happening to your family and friends. Getting everyone on the same page right away is key to avoiding accidental cross-contamination later. In our house, which is all gluten and dairy free, we have a cupboard and a contained area in the refrigerator for any gluten- or dairy-containing items that make it into our house. Condiments in the refrigerator that may contain dairy are very clearly marked and kept in their own space. Dairy milks that may be in the house should be stored on the bottom shelf of the refrigerator to prevent any accidental dripping on the dairy-free items in the fridge.

ELECTRICAL GADGETS

High-powered Blender

Of all the tools in my dairy-free kitchen, this is the one I use the most. With a high-powered blender, I can grind frozen fruits into creamy dairy-free smoothies, pulverize nuts into smooth mixtures to create dairy-free cheeses, blend personalized versions of dairy-free milks and concoct silky sauces all without dairy. Be sure to look for a blender that has a powerful motor, variable speed control and a pulse feature.

Heavy-duty Stand Mixer

Many shop-bought baked goods contain dairy and dairy-free options are not available in-store. You will need to make certain treats at home if you would like to enjoy them, so I consider a great stand mixer a must for every dairy-free kitchen. Some brands of stand mixers have attachments that make them even more useful in the dairy-free kitchen, such as an ice-cream maker, or food processing attachments. Try not to skimp on your mixer and get the one with the sturdiest motor that you can afford. Keep an eye out for sales to help stretch your budget.

Stick (Immersion) Blender or Hand-held Blender

I use this often to blend ingredients right in the pan for everything from dairy-free cream-based soups to cheese sauces. I even use it to whip up our eggs before scrambling them. Blending hot liquids can be dangerous in a blender, causing the lid to pop off and scalding liquid to spill everywhere, but this little tool can smooth out a sauce right on the hob (stove), eliminating that risk.

Yogurt Maker

When I realized my dairy-free family went through more dairy-free yogurt than our budget could comfortably handle, I bought a yogurt maker to make my own. At the time, there were also not very many dairy-free yogurts on the market and I wanted to change the types of dairy-free milks we made our yogurt from and avoid the additives in the shop-bought varieties. It is fun to try different milk combinations and to blend up our own flavours. Look for a yogurt maker with a variable temperature control and an automatic shut-off switch.

MILK AND CHEESE MAKING

A Nut Milk Bag

Even finer than the finest muslin (*see* page 54), nut milk bags are an essential tool to strain out homemade dairy-free milk. Look online to purchase one or check your local

health-food store. Nut milk bags are reusable, easy to clean and dry quickly. They can also be used to strain juice!

Butter Muslin or Cheesecloth

Found in most supermarkets, ordinary muslin (cheesecloth) with a very loose weave will not be as useful for dairy-free cheese-making, so look for one with smaller holes that will hold your mixture together while allowing excess liquid to drain. This type of muslin is traditionally used to line cheese moulds, aiding in cheese production by drawing the moisture from the cheese curds to the drain holes of the cheese mould. Butter muslin, however, is a much finer weave than ordinary muslin or cheesecloth, making it ideal to drain dairy-free yogurts to make a thicker Greek-style yogurt or when making dairy-free cream cheese. Butter muslin can be used in a pinch to strain homemade dairy-free milks if you do not have a nut milk bag.

COOKING POTS & BAKING SHEETS

Unfortunately, these can be a major source of cross-contamination. The big tip for deciding if you need to replace any of your cookware: if it is made of a porous material, such as cast iron or stoneware, it will need to be replaced, as there is no effective way of completely removing dairy allergens for those who are highly allergic. Any baking sheets or baking tins (pans) that have a built up layer of 'seasoning' made from baking with butter or cheese items should also be replaced. Inspect stainless steel tins carefully for a layer of burnt oil build-up. Stainless steel can be scoured until it is shiny and new-looking.

STAPLES

PLANT-BASED MILKS

While you can always buy dairy-free milks, making your own allows you to control the consistency, flavour and ingredients. You can also custom-blend your favourite combinations, such as coconut and macadamia or hazelnut and hemp milk.

Makes 710 ml–1 litre/ 1½–1¾ pints/ 3–4 cups

Choose one or a combination of

350 g/12 oz/2 cups desiccated (shredded unsweetened) coconut

165 g/5½ oz/1 cup cooked rice or millet

75 g/3 oz/½ cup hulled hemp seeds

125 g/4 oz/1 cup raw cashews

100 g/3½ oz/1 cup rolled oats

130 g/4½ oz/1 cup raw sunflower seeds

150 g/5 oz/1 cup raw nuts, such as almonds, hazelnuts, macadamia, walnuts, Brazil nuts, pecans, etc.

To make milk

1 litre/1¾ pints/4 cups water (use less water for thicker, creamier milk)

dash salt

Optional mix-ins

1–2 dates or 1–1½ tbsp, or to taste, maple syrup, honey or brown rice syrup, to sweeten

25 g/1 oz/¼ cup berries

3–4 tbsp cocoa powder

½–1 tsp vanilla extract

½ tsp ground cinnamon

To make milk, there's no need to presoak coconut, cooked rice or hemp seeds. If making milk from cashews, put the nuts in a bowl and cover with water at least 2.5 cm/1 inch deep and soak for 3 hours. If making milk from oats, sunflower seeds, or other nuts, soak in water overnight.

When ready to make the milk, drain the ingredients, discarding the soaking water, then place the seeds or nuts in a high-powered blender with the 1 litre/1¾ pints/4 cups water and salt and blitz until almost smooth. If using dates to sweeten, or making berry milk, blend them with the seeds or nuts and water.

Using a nut milk bag or butter muslin (cheesecloth) or other clean, tightly woven cloth, strain the blended mixture into a container. Twist the cloth tightly to squeeze out all remaining milk.

Pour about one-quarter of the milk into a saucepan and heat, whisking until the mixture just about begins to boil, but do not let it actually come to the boil. Keep stirring until thickened, which will happen very quickly once it becomes hot enough. Remove from the heat and whisk in the remaining milk. This step will help keep the milk from separating while it is stored.

If using cocoa, vanilla or cinnamon, stir them in now. Cover and refrigerate. The milk will keep for 3–4 days.

FIRM CASHEW NUT CHEESE

This cheese is delicious and wonderfully versatile. Firm cashew nut cheese can be sliced or grated and melts well in a toasted sandwich.

Serves 6

125 g/4 oz/1 cup raw cashews

10 g/¼ oz/¼ cup nutritional yeast flakes or 2 tbsp nutritional yeast powder

50 ml/2 fl oz/¼ cup lemon juice

1 tsp white miso paste

1½ tsp onion powder

1 tsp salt

½ tsp garlic powder

2 tsp agar powder or 2 tbsp agar flakes or 2 tbsp powdered gelatine
   or 2 tsp psyllium powder

oil, for oiling

Put the cashews in a bowl and cover with water at least 2.5 cm/1 inch deep over the nuts. Cover with plastic wrap and soak overnight. When ready to make the cheese, drain and rinse the cashews.

Put the cashews, nutritional yeast, lemon juice, miso paste, onion powder, salt and garlic powder into a high-powdered blender and blend until smooth.

If using agar, bring 350 ml/12 fl oz/1½ cups water to the boil and add the agar. While stirring constantly, boil for 1 minute, then reduce the heat and simmer for another 5 minutes.

If using gelatine, put 120 ml/4 fl oz/½ cup water into a small bowl and sprinkle over the gelatine. Leave for 1 minute until the gelatine rehydrates (or 'blooms'). Put the remaining water in a small saucepan and bring to the boil. Add the gelatine mixture and stir until it has dissolved.

Immediately after preparing the agar or gelatine mixture, pour into the blender with the cashew mixture and carefully blend. Hot mixtures in a blender can cause the lid to pop off. Using oven gloves, hold down the lid and blend until very smooth, scraping down the sides of the blender as needed.

Pour the mixture into an oiled container, cover and chill until firm. Store in the refrigerator for up to 5 days.

Sliceable Cheese Without Cashews

Steam 200 g/7 oz/2 cups cauliflower and 4 garlic cloves until very tender. Meanwhile, sprinkle 3 tbsp powdered gelatine over 50 ml/2 fl oz/¼ cup canned full-fat coconut milk. When the gelatine has rehydrated (bloomed), put into a high-powered blender with the cauliflower and garlic, 4 tbsp nutritional yeast flakes, 3 tbsp tapioca flour (starch), 1 tsp salt, or more to taste, 2 tbsp coconut oil, 2 tbsp coconut cream, 2 tsp lemon juice or cider vinegar and ½ tsp ground turmeric. Blend until very smooth, scraping down the sides of the blender, if needed. Pour the mixture into a saucepan and cook over a medium heat for 7 minutes, or until it thickens. Pour into an oiled container, cover and chill until firm.

COTTAGE CHEESE

This recipe works best with purchased plant-based milks, as it contains emulsifiers to help keep it from separating. To test if homemade plant-based milk will work, pour 120 ml/4 fl oz/$\frac{1}{2}$ cup dairy-free milk and add $\frac{1}{2}$ tsp cider vinegar or lemon juice. Leave for a few minutes and check to see if the milk is starting to curdle. If it is, you will be able to use it to make cottage cheese.

Serves 4-6

1 litre/1¾ pints/4 cups shop-bought sweetened coconut, almond or soy milk
4 tbsp lemon juice or cider vinegar
2 tsp olive oil
salt

Pour the milk into a saucepan and bring to a gentle boil, stirring frequently. Remove from the heat and add the lemon juice or vinegar, stirring well. The mixture should curdle and separate.

Using butter muslin (cheesecloth), strain the mixture into a bowl, saving the liquid. You may need to stir a little of the strained liquid back into the curds, so the cottage cheese will not be too dry.

When the curds are drained, put into a bowl and stir in the oil and a little of the reserved liquid, if needed, to get to the desired texture. Add salt to taste. Cover and store in the refrigerator for up to 1 week.

RICOTTA

This recipe can easily be cut in half or doubled if you need a larger amount of ricotta for a recipe.

Makes about 450 g/1 lb/2 cups

275 g/10 oz/2 cups raw pine nuts or raw cashews

2 tbsp lemon juice

2 tbsp nutritional yeast flakes or 1 tbsp nutritional yeast powder

1 tsp salt, or to taste

Put the nuts in a bowl and cover with water at least 2.5 cm/1 inch deep over the nuts. Soak for 2–3 hours. Drain and rinse.

Pulse the nuts, lemon juice, nutritional yeast and salt in a food processor or blender until it is fluffy but still has some texture, scraping down the sides of the food processor as needed.

If needed, add a small amount of water a little at a time to achieve the desired texture.

MOZZARELLA

Mozzarella can be shaped into small pearls for starters or into larger balls for slicing and adding to a caprese salad, for instance, or for melting in sandwiches or on pizza.

Makes about 350 g / 12 oz / 1½ cups or 3 medium mozzarella balls

165 g/5½ oz/1⅓ cups raw cashews or pine nuts
2 tbsp lemon juice
3 tbsp psyllium powder
1 tsp white miso paste

3 tbsp nutritional yeast flakes or
  1½ tbsp nutritional yeast powder
salt
oil, for oiling (optional)

Put the cashews or pine nuts in a bowl and cover with water at least 2.5 cm/1 inch deep over the nuts. Soak overnight. When ready to make the cheese, drain and rinse.

Mix 200 ml/7 fl oz/¾ cup water, lemon juice and psyllium powder together in a small bowl. Leave for at least 1 hour until the mixture has gelled and is very thick. Alternatively, cover with plastic wrap and soak overnight while the nuts are soaking.

Put the nuts, psyllium mixture, miso paste and nutritional yeast into a high-powered blender and mix until very smooth. Taste and add salt to taste, mixing in well. Pour the mixture into oiled round containers or wrap small amounts of the mixture in squares of plastic wrap, twisting to form traditionally shaped balls. Chill for at least 1 hour or until firm and sliceable.

Nut-free Version

Whisk together 175 ml/6 fl oz/scant ¾ cup canned coconut milk, 1½ tsp olive oil or refined coconut oil, 1½ tsp lemon juice or cider vinegar, 1½ tsp nutritional yeast flakes and ½ tsp salt in a saucepan over a medium heat until warm. In a small bowl, whisk 4½ tbsp water and 4½ tbsp tapioca flour (starch) together, pour into the pan and heat, whisking until it thickens and begins to pull away from the sides. Remove from the heat and shape. Chill for 2 hours, or until firm.

GOAT`S CHEESE

Overnight fermentation helps develop the flavour of this cheese to mimic the taste of goat's cheese. Creamy, yet crumbly, it is perfect for sprinkling into salads or spreading on toast. Feel free to add herbs or spices after the cheese has fermented, but before chilling.

Makes about 250 g/8 oz/1 cup

125 g/4 oz/1 cup raw cashews

65 g/2½ oz/½ cup macadamia nuts or pine nuts

1½ tbsp lemon juice

1 tbsp cider vinegar

½ tbsp white miso paste

½ tsp salt, or to taste

about 2–4 tbsp water

Put the nuts in a bowl and cover with water at least 2.5 cm/1 inch deep over the nuts. Soak overnight. When ready to make the cheese, drain and rinse the nuts.

Blend the soaked nuts, lemon juice, vinegar, miso paste and salt together in a high-powered blender until smooth. Add the water, 1 tbsp at a time, blending between additions, to create a thick, mouldable cheese.

Shape the mixture into a log on plastic wrap or in another clean container. Cover and leave at room temperature overnight to develop the flavour.

The next day, put the cheese in the refrigerator. It can be sliced after chilling with a thin, sharp knife.

PARMESAN

You don't have to miss out on your favourite topping any more! This is so good sprinkled on spaghetti, pizza and popcorn.

Makes about 175 g/6 oz/³/₄ cup

100 g/3½ oz/1 cup blanched flaked (slivered) almonds,
   raw cashews or macadamia nuts
1½ tbsp nutritional yeast flakes or ¾ tbsp nutritional yeast powder
½–1 tsp salt, or to taste
¼ tsp onion powder
¼ tsp garlic powder

Put all the ingredients into a food processor and pulse until the mixture is ground into a powder. Cover and store in the refrigerator for up to 3 weeks, or place in a freezerproof container and freeze for longer storage.

Dairy-free Parmesan You Can Grate

After pulsing the mixture to a powder, add 2½ tsp lemon juice and 1¼ tsp rice wine vinegar. Blend until it comes together and is smooth. Shape into a ball and flatten to about 2.5 cm/ 1 inch thick. Cover in plastic wrap and chill for several hours or overnight until firm.

Dairy-free Parmesan Without Nuts

Put 225 g/8 oz/1¼cups desiccated (unsweetened shredded) coconut into a high-powered blender and blend on high speed, scraping down as needed, until smooth and liquefied. Add 1½ tbsp lemon juice, 10 g/¼ oz/¼ cup nutritional yeast flakes, ¼ tsp ascorbic acid (vitamin C crystals) and ½ tsp salt and blend again. Slowly drizzle in 100 g/3½ oz/½ cup melted coconut oil, blending until well incorporated and very smooth. Pour into a container and chill until firm. Grate when cold, as this substitute will soften due to the coconut content.

SWISS CHEESE

This cheese is fabulous served on a burger with sautéed mushrooms, or grated in a quiche. Try a Swiss cheese and ham melt sandwich or add to an omelette with asparagus and caramelized shallots.

Makes about 450 g/1 lb/2 cups

65 g/2½ oz/½ cup raw Brazil nuts, macadamia nuts, or blanched almonds

350 ml/12 fl oz/1½ cups water

10 g/¼ oz/¼ cup nutritional yeast flakes or 2 tbsp nutritional yeast powder

3 tbsp lemon juice

2 tbsp tahini or 1 tbsp white miso paste

¾ tsp dry mustard powder

½ tsp onion powder

½ tsp salt, or to taste

¼ tsp garlic powder

1½ tbsp agar powder or 3 tbsp powdered gelatine

Put the nuts in a bowl and cover with water at least 2.5 cm/1 inch deep over the nuts. Soak overnight. When ready to make the cheese, drain and rinse.

Blend the nuts, 120 ml4 fl oz/½ cup of the water, the nutritional yeast, lemon juice, tahini, dry mustard powder, onion powder, salt and garlic powder together in a high-powered blender until smooth.

If using agar, bring the remaining water to the boil and add the agar. While stirring constantly, boil for 1 minute, then reduce the heat and simmer for another 5 minutes.

If using gelatine, put the 120 ml/4 fl oz/½ cup water into a small bowl and sprinkle over the gelatine. Leave for 1 minute until the gelatine rehydrates (blooms). Put the remaining water in a small saucepan and bring to the boil. Add the gelatine mixture and stir until it has dissolved.

Immediately after preparing the agar or gelatine mixture, pour into the blender with the cashew mixture and carefully blend. Hot mixtures in a blender can cause the lid to pop off. Using oven gloves, hold down the lid and blend until very smooth, scraping down the sides of the blender as needed.

Pour into a container, cover and chill for 4 hours, or until firm. For a more traditional look, poke straws of various sizes through the finished cheese to make holes before slicing.

YOGURT

Dairy-free yogurt needs help to thicken, unlike dairy-based yogurts. You can use tapioca, as here, or use 2 tsp powdered gelatine sprinkled on the coconut milk before heating. The sugar is used to feed the yogurt culture, so do include it. Don't replace it with honey, as honey has natural antibacterial properties that will compete with the culture.

Makes about 875 ml/1³/₄ pints/3½ cups

2 tbsp tapioca flour (starch)

1 tsp sugar, maple syrup or sweetener of choice

875 ml/1¾ pints/3½ cups unsweetened dairy-free milk of choice, canned full-fat coconut milk or homemade nut or seed milk

50 ml/2 fl oz/¼ cup plain dairy-free yogurt, or 4 probiotic capsules, or dairy-free yogurt starter of choice

Make sure all the yogurt equipment is clean and sterilized. Whisk the tapioca flour (starch) and sugar together in a saucepan. Whisk in the milk and heat, whisking frequently until thickened and starting to simmer. Remove from the heat. Cool the mixture until it is 43°C/110°F or the temperature needed for a yogurt starter.

Whisk the yogurt, the contents of the probiotic capsules, or the starter into the milk until well combined. Pour the mixture into sterilized jars and incubate in the yogurt maker for 12 hours. Once culturing is complete, put the lids on the containers and put the jars in the refrigerator. The yogurt will thicken when it cools.

To Incubate Without a Yogurt Maker...

Pour the mixture into a 1.1 litre/2 pint/1 quart sterilized canning jar with a lid. Place in a cooler with 2 or 3 canning jars filled with boiling water and separated with tea towels. Shut the cooler and leave to incubate for 12 hours. Do not peek during this time or it will release crucial heat.

BUTTERY SPREAD

This dairy-free buttery spread is wonderful spread on toast, slathered on pancakes or as a topping on a baked potato. Use refined coconut oil in this recipe, as unrefined coconut oil tastes of coconut.

Makes 250 g / 8 oz / 1 cup

2½ tbsp canned full-fat coconut milk

2 tbsp mild-flavoured unsweetened dairy-free milk of choice

1 tsp cider vinegar

¼ tsp salt, or to taste

10½ tbsp refined coconut oil, melted but close to room temperature

1 tbsp extra virgin olive oil, sunflower oil, corn oil or buttery-tasting oil of choice

1 tsp liquid sunflower lecithin, psyllium powder or deodorized cocoa butter

¼ tsp xanthan or guar gum

Whisk both milks, the vinegar and salt together in a small bowl. Leave for 5–10 minutes.

Put the coconut oil and olive oil into a food processor or blender, add the coconut milk mixture, lecithin and xanthan gum and process for 2 minutes, or until the mixture is well blended and emulsified.

Put the mixture into a freezerproof container and freeze for at least 1 hour, or overnight, until firm. The mixture needs to chill as quickly as possible to stay blended. Remove from the freezer when firm. Put into an airtight container and store in the refrigerator for up to one month.

Note

Deodorized cocoa butter is lighter in scent than ordinary cocoa butter.

HAZELNUT CHOCOLATE SPREAD

Most commercial hazelnut chocolate spreads contain dairy, so this recipe is a great replacement. It's easy to make, with all the flavour you crave.

Makes 250 g/8 oz/1 cup

130 g/4½ oz/1 cup raw hazelnuts

275 g/10 oz/2 cups dairy-free dark (bittersweet, or half bittersweet and half semisweet) chocolate, chopped

2 tbsp mild-flavoured oil, plus extra if needed

3 tbsp icing (confectioners') sugar

1 tbsp cocoa powder

½ tsp vanilla extract

½ tsp salt

Preheat the oven to 180°C/350°F/Gas Mark 4. Spread the hazelnuts out in a single layer on a rimmed baking sheet and toast for 12–14 minutes until they have darkened and the skins have blistered. Allow to cool slightly. Wrap the nuts in a clean tea towel and rub to remove as much of the skin as possible. Cool completely.

Place the chocolate in a heatproof bowl set over a pan of gently simmering water, making sure the base of the bowl doesn't touch the water, and heat until the chocolate has almost melted. Turn off the heat and stir until smooth. Allow to cool slightly.

Grind the cooled hazelnuts in a high-powered blender or food processor until they form a paste. Add the oil, sugar, cocoa powder, vanilla extract and salt and continue to process, scraping down the sides of the blender as needed, until very smooth. Blend in the melted chocolate, then transfer to a bowl and cool. It will thicken as it cools. If needed, blend in a little more oil to keep it a spreadable texture.

Transfer the spread to a container, cover and store in the refrigerator for up to one month. Allow to come to room temperature before using.

WHIPPED COCONUT CREAM

I leave a couple of cans of coconut cream in my refrigerator at all times. You never know when you might want to whip up a creamy topping for hot chocolate, a latte or a freshly baked pie.

Makes about 350 ml/12 fl oz/1½ cups

400 ml/14 fl oz can full-fat coconut milk or coconut cream, with the highest fat
   content you can find, chilled overnight
½ tsp vanilla extract
dash salt
25–50 g/1–2 oz/¼–½ cup icing (confectioners') sugar, or to taste

Remove the chilled coconut milk or cream from the refrigerator, being careful not to tip or shake it. Open the can and scoop out only the thickened cream at the top, leaving the remaining liquid for another recipe, such as a smoothie or curry. You should have a minimum of 250 g/9 oz/1 cup coconut cream.

Using an ice-cold bowl and beaters, whip the cold cream for 30 seconds. Add the vanilla, salt and icing (confectioners') sugar and beat for 1–2 minutes until fluffy and smooth.

Chocolate Whipped Coconut Cream

Add 25 g/1 oz/¼ cup sifted cocoa powder to the cream when adding the icing sugar.

Stabilized Whipped Coconut Cream

Sprinkle 1 tsp unflavoured powdered gelatine over 4 tsp cold water. Leave until the gelatine has rehydrated (bloomed), then heat until just melted. Allow to cool slightly, but not gel. After the icing sugar is added to the cream, put the mixer on low and drizzle in the melted gelatine. Increase the speed of the mixer and beat until fluffy.

VANILLA ICE CREAM

To make a custard-style ice cream, replace tapioca flour (starch) with two beaten medium (large) eggs, adding the eggs to the coconut milk mixture before heating. Strain the mixture through a sieve (strainer) before cooling and continue with the recipe below.

Makes about 450 g/1 lb/1 pint

100 g/3½ oz/¾ cup sugar

2 tbsp tapioca flour (starch), cornflour (cornstarch) or arrowroot

720 ml/1¼ pints/3 cups canned coconut milk or half coconut milk and half milk substitute of choice, such as almond milk

2 tsp vanilla extract

Whisk the sugar and tapioca flour (starch) together in a medium saucepan. Whisk in the milk substitute(s) and heat over a medium heat, whisking frequently until the sugar has dissolved. Do not boil. The mixture will thicken slightly.

Allow to cool to room temperature, then stir in the vanilla extract. Cover and cool in the refrigerator until chilled.

When cooled, put the mixture into an ice-cream maker and freeze according to the manufacturer's instructions. For a firmer texture, place the ice cream in a freezerproof container, cover and freeze for about 2 hours.

Variations

Use the basic vanilla recipe as a template to create your favourite ice cream flavours. Unless otherwise stated, flavourings should be added before chilling and putting in ice-cream maker. Mix-ins, such as nuts, raisins and chocolate chips, should be stirred in after freezing in the ice-cream maker.

Banana: Mash a very ripe banana and add to the mixture with the vanilla. After processing, stir in 50 g/2 oz/½ cup toasted pecans or 25 g/1 oz/¼ cup toasted pecans and 40 g/1½ oz/¼ cup dairy-free chocolate chips.

Chocolate and Choc Chip: Whisk 50 g/2 oz/½ cup cocoa powder into the sugar and tapioca flour mixture. And/or, after processing, stir in 65 g/2½ oz/⅓ cup dairy-free mini chocolate chips.

Coffee: Add 2 tbsp instant coffee to the sugar and tapioca flour mixture.

Cookies 'n' Cream: After processing the vanilla ice cream, stir in 50 g/2 oz/½ cup crushed dairy-free cookies of choice.

Maple Walnut: Replace 50 g/2 oz/¼ cup sugar with 75 g/3 oz/¼ cup maple syrup. After processing, stir in 65 g/2½ oz/½ cup toasted walnuts.

HOT FUDGE SAUCE

This is wonderful poured over any flavour of dairy-free ice cream. Decadent, thick and delicious, it is very simple to make and so much better than shop-bought. Try it drizzled over strawberries or use cooled as a fudge layer in a cake.

Makes about 600 ml/1 pint/2½ cups

50 g/2 oz/¼ cup coconut oil or dairy-free Buttery Spread (*see* page 78), or half of each
250 ml/8 fl oz/1 cup full-fat canned coconut milk, stir until smooth before measuring
225 g/8 oz/1 cup (packed) brown sugar
75 g/3 oz/⅓ cup caster (superfine) sugar
100 g/3½ oz/1 cup cocoa powder, sifted
¼ tsp salt
1 tsp vanilla extract

Whisk the coconut oil and coconut milk together in a saucepan over a medium heat. When the oil has melted, add the sugars, cocoa powder and salt and whisk well until completely blended. Continue to heat until the mixture is very smooth without any sugar crystals remaining, whisking frequently, then simmer for 1 minute, whisking constantly. Add the vanilla extract, whisking to combine, then remove from the heat.

Serve over dairy-free ice cream or anywhere hot fudge could be served. To store, place in a heatproof container, such as a canning jar. Allow to cool to room temperature, then cover and refrigerate. To reheat, put the uncovered jar in a saucepan with water partway up the side of the jar and heat to your desired temperature.

SAUCES, DIPS & DRESSINGS

BÉCHAMEL SAUCE

Béchamel sauce is a classic with so many uses. Use the creamy sauce as it is, or add herbs, spices, garlic or cooked diced mushrooms.

Makes 500 ml/18 fl oz/2 cups

3 tbsp mild-flavoured olive oil
2 tbsp flour or 1 tbsp cornflour (cornstarch)
500 ml/18 fl oz/2 cups unsweetened dairy-free milk of choice, such as almond
salt

Heat the oil in a pan over a medium heat. Sprinkle the flour or cornflour (cornstarch) into the oil and whisk to combine, then cook the flour in the oil, whisking constantly. Do not allow the flour to scorch or burn. Reduce the heat if the mixture begins to stick to the pan.

While continuing to whisk, slowly add the milk. Continue to cook while whisking until the mixture is thickened. Season with salt to taste.

CHEDDAR CHEESE SAUCE
with Nacho Variation

A delicious sauce that can be made milder or spicier, depending on how you like it, by adjusting how much chilli powder and jalapeños you add. Drizzle over nachos or use as a dip for vegetables or chips.

Makes 720 ml/1¼ pints/3 cups

125 g/4 oz/1 cup raw cashews

500 ml/18 fl oz/2 cups water

50 g/2 oz jar pimentos, drained

40 g/1½ oz/1 cup nutritional yeast flakes or
    25 g/1 oz/½ cup nutritional yeast powder

2 tbsp cornflour (cornstarch)

1 tbsp lemon juice

1½ tsp salt, or to taste

½ tsp onion powder

¼ tsp garlic powder

For the nacho variation

½ tsp ground cumin

½ tsp dried oregano

¼ tsp chilli powder or chipotle
    chilli powder

75 g/3 oz/⅓ cup drained salsa

To garnish (optional)

2 tbsp chopped jalapeño chilli (pepper)

1 tbsp chopped coriander (cilantro)

Blend the cashews to a fine powder in a blender. Add the remaining ingredients and blend until completely smooth. Transfer the mixture to a medium saucepan and whisk constantly over a medium heat for 5–6 minutes until thickened. If using, stir in the 'nacho variation' ingredients at this point. Sprinkle with chilli and coriander (cilantro), if liked, and serve hot.

Nut-free Sauce

In a blender, blend 500 ml/18 fl oz/2 cups unsweetened dairy-free milk of choice, 50 g/2 oz jar drained pimentos, 2½ tbsp cornflour (cornstarch), 1½ tbsp olive oil, 1 tbsp lemon juice, 1½ tsp salt, ½ tsp each onion powder and garlic powder until smooth. Transfer the mixture to a saucepan and cook as above. Makes about 500 ml/18 fl oz/2 cups.

CLASSIC PESTO

Pesto is a savoury bite of summer, packed with basil and garlic. Toss with pasta as a sauce, brush on a baguette and top with dairy-free mozzarella, or brush on chicken or fish.

Makes about 225 g / 8 oz / 1 cup

50 g/2 oz/2 cups (packed) basil leaves, stems removed

3 tbsp pine nuts, walnuts, pumpkin seeds or sunflower seeds

3 large garlic cloves, peeled

2 tbsp lemon juice

3 tbsp nutritional yeast flakes or 1½ tbsp nutritional yeast powder

¼ tsp salt, or more to taste

2–3 tbsp extra virgin olive oil

3–6 tbsp water, as much as needed to reach desired consistency

Pulse the basil, nuts, garlic, lemon juice, nutritional yeast and ¼ tsp salt in a food processor or blender until chopped.

While the machine is still running, drizzle the olive oil into the mixture, scraping down the sides of the food processor as needed. Add the water, 1 tbsp at a time, until your desired consistency is reached. The pesto should be thick, yet pourable.

Taste and adjust the seasoning if necessary. Add a bit more nutritional yeast if you prefer a cheesier flavour, garlic for more bite, lemon juice for brightness, or more salt, if needed. Store any leftovers covered in the refrigerator for up to a week or freeze in an ice-cube tray for longer storage.

CAULIFLOWER ALFREDO SAUCE

Not just for pasta, this dreamy sauce can be drizzled on steamed vegetables, used as a creamy sauce for crisp roasted fish or stirred into a casserole.

Makes 500 ml/18 fl oz/2 cups

1 tbsp olive or coconut oil

½ onion, peeled and chopped

3 garlic cloves, peeled and crushed

300 g/11 oz/3 cups cauliflower, chopped

250 ml/8 fl oz/1 cup unsweetened dairy-free milk, or chicken or vegetable stock or water

1–2 tbsp nutritional yeast flakes

½ tbsp lemon juice

½ tsp salt, or to taste

½ tsp tamari sauce

freshly ground black pepper

Heat the oil in a medium pan over a medium-high heat, add the onion and cook until translucent and tender. Add the garlic and cook for about 30 seconds.

Add the cauliflower and milk, then reduce the heat to medium and bring to a light simmer, stirring occasionally. When the milk is lightly simmering, cover and steam for 4–5 minutes until tender.

Transfer the contents of the pan to a blender, add the remaining ingredients and blend until smooth. Alternatively, add the remaining ingredients to the pan and blend until smooth with a stick blender. Use the sauce straightaway or return to the pan over a low heat to keep warm until ready to serve.

TZATZIKI

Creamy with zesty garlic and cooling cucumber, tzatziki is the perfect condiment to serve with lamb, chicken, fish or falafels.

Makes about 700 g / 1½ lb / 3 cups

1 cucumber, coarsely grated (in the US, the 'English' type is the best to use)

1 tsp salt

500 ml/18 fl oz/2 cups unsweetened plain dairy-free yogurt

3 garlic cloves, peeled and very finely chopped

1 tbsp extra virgin olive oil

1 tbsp lemon juice

1 tsp white wine vinegar

½ tsp lemon zest

1 tbsp very finely chopped dill or 1 tsp dried dill

freshly ground black pepper

Sprinkle the cucumber with the salt and toss. Set aside for 30 minutes to drain, then squeeze any excess moisture from the cucumbers.

Whisk the yogurt, garlic, olive oil, lemon juice, vinegar, lemon zest, dill and black pepper together in a small bowl.

Stir the drained cucumbers into the yogurt mixture, cover and chill until ready to serve.

TAHINI DRESSING

A quick dressing that's perfect on salad, grains or roasted vegetables.

Makes about 250 ml/ 8 fl oz/ 1 cup

125 g/4 oz/1½ cup tahini

120 ml/4 fl oz/½ cup red wine vinegar

juice of 1 lemon

1 tsp dried oregano

¼ tsp garlic powder

salt and freshly ground black pepper

Whisk all the ingredients together in a bowl. Add a little water if needed to thin the dressing to your desired consistency.

Cover and chill until ready to serve. Whisk again if needed before serving.

RANCH DRESSING

My family's all-time favourite dip and salad dressing, it is also a perfect topper for baked potatoes.

Makes about 315 ml/ 11 fl oz/ 1¹/₃ cups

175 g/6 oz/scant ¾ cup dairy-free mayonnaise

40 g/11½ oz/⅓ cup very finely chopped celery, including leaves

2 tbsp very finely chopped parsley or 2 tsp dried parsley

1 tbsp very finely chopped yellow onion

1 tsp lemon juice or cider vinegar

1 garlic clove, peeled and crushed

¼ tsp dried thyme

¼ tsp celery seed

⅛ tsp salt, or to taste

⅛ tsp freshly ground black pepper, or to taste

2–4 tbsp unsweetened dairy-free milk of choice

Combine all the ingredients, except the milk, together in a bowl. Mix in the milk, a little at a time, until the dressing is thin enough to pour.

Cover and chill until ready to serve. Whisk again if needed before serving.

LEMON & POPPY SEED DRESSING

This dressing is light and is the perfect balance of tangy and sweet to go on all your summer salads, such as salads topped with berries or peaches.

Makes about 500 ml/18 fl oz/2 cups

350 ml/12 fl oz/1½ cups light-flavoured vegetable or mild-flavoured olive oil

200 ml/7 fl oz/¾ cup white wine vinegar

150 g/5 oz/¾ cup granulated sugar

2 tbsp finely chopped onion

1 tsp salt, or to taste

¾ tsp dry mustard powder

1½ tbsp poppy seeds

Place all the ingredients, except the poppy seeds, in a blender. Blend on high for about 1 minute, or until the dressing is completely emulsified and the sugar has dissolved. Stir in the poppy seeds.

Chill before using. Whisk again if needed before serving.

BLUE CHEESE DIP

This dairy-free dip is just the thing to serve with spicy buffalo wings and celery, or thinned and served on an iceberg wedge salad.

Makes about 300 ml/10 fl oz/1¼ cups

50 g/2 oz/¼ cup raw cashews

225 g/8 oz/1 cup dairy-free mayonnaise

1½ tsp tahini

1 tsp cider vinegar

½ tsp lemon juice

½ tsp salt

¼ tsp garlic powder

freshly ground black pepper

Put the nuts in a bowl and cover with warm water at least 2.5 cm/1 inch deep over the nuts. Soak for at least 2 hours, then drain and rinse.

Mix the mayonnaise, tahini, vinegar, lemon juice, salt, garlic powder and black pepper together in a bowl. Put the cashews and the mayonnaise mixture into a food processor or blender and pulse until the cashews are chopped into small pieces, but not blended completely smooth.

Cover and chill until ready to serve.

Note

To turn this into a dressing, add enough unsweetened dairy-free milk of choice to the dip until the dressing is the desired consistency.

DRINKS & SMOOTHIES

GOLDEN MILK

Golden milk has become a staple in our home. We drink it in the evening as a soothing, warm beverage before bed.

Serves 2

1 tsp ground turmeric

¼ tsp ground cinnamon

¼ tsp ground ginger

¼ tsp ground cardamom

dash freshly ground black pepper

500 ml/18 fl oz/2 cups coconut milk

2 tbsp honey or maple syrup

½ tsp vanilla extract

Whisk the turmeric, cinnamon, ginger, cardamom and black pepper together in a saucepan. Slowly add the milk, whisking to combine. Heat over a medium heat until steaming.

Remove from the heat, stir in the honey and vanilla extract, then pour into mugs to serve.

BERRY SMOOTHIE

If your prefer an even thicker, frostier smoothie, use frozen berries instead of fresh.

Serves 1

100 g/3½ oz/1 cup strawberries

25 g/1 oz/¼ cup blueberries

25 g/1 oz/¼ cup blackberries

1 chopped banana, frozen

120 ml/4 fl oz/½ cup dairy-free yogurt, or dairy-free milk of choice mixed
   with ½ tsp lemon juice

½ tbsp honey

unsweetened dairy-free milk of choice (optional)

Put all the ingredients into a high-powered blender and blend until smooth,
adding a little milk if it's too thick.

BANANA CREAM PIE SMOOTHIE

Cool and creamy, like banana cream pie in a glass!

Serves 1

1 sliced banana, frozen

120 ml/4 fl oz/½ cup unsweetened dairy-free milk of choice

50 ml/2 fl oz/¼ cup dairy-free yogurt, or dairy-free milk of choice mixed with
½ tsp lemon juice

2 tbsp dairy-free digestive biscuit crumbs (Graham cracker crumbs without
chocolate coating), plus extra to serve

1½ tsp honey

1 tsp vanilla extract

¼ tsp ground cinnamon

⅛ tsp ground nutmeg

4–5 ice cubes (½ cup)

2 slices banana, to serve

Place all the ingredients into a high-powered blender and blend until very smooth.
Pour into a glass and sprinkle with extra digestive biscuit (cracker) crumbs and
2 slices of banana.

MASALA CHAI

It takes a few more minutes and steps to make authentic masala chai instead of using a ready-made blend, but it is definitely worth it. Sweet, spicy and creamy, this tea is wonderfully comforting. I often double or triple this and make a larger batch to enjoy all week. After straining, cover, cool, then refrigerate. Stir, pour and enjoy cold or warm.

Serves 2

5 cm/2 inch cinnamon stick, broken up

15 black peppercorns

½ star anise

5 cloves

5 green cardamom pods, crushed, or ½ tsp cardamom seeds, crushed

500 ml/18 fl oz/2 cups water

2 pieces crystallized ginger, chopped, or 2 cm/¾ inch piece grated for a more intense ginger flavour

3 tsp loose, strong black tea leaves

350 ml/12 fl oz/1½ cups unsweetened dairy-free milk, such as coconut or almond

2 tbsp honey or maple syrup, or to taste

Toast the cinnamon stick, peppercorns, star anise, cloves and cardamom pods in a pan over a low heat for 1–2 minutes until very fragrant. Add the water and ginger and bring to the boil over a medium-high heat. Lower the heat and simmer for 20 minutes, or until the liquid is reduced by one third.

Remove from the heat and add the tea leaves. Allow to steep for 2 minutes. Add the milk and honey, to taste. Return to the heat and bring to a simmer, whisking frequently for about 5 minutes. After a simmer is reached, steep for another 5 minutes, then strain and serve.

GREEN YOGURT SMOOTHIE

Start your day with dairy-free creaminess – sweet banana with the nutritional punch of spinach and avocado.

Serves 1

1 frozen banana, broken into chunks

25 g/1 oz/1 cup baby spinach leaves or chopped kale, stems removed

120 ml/4 fl oz/½ cup dairy-free yogurt

½ ripe avocado, pitted and peeled

120 ml/4 fl oz/½ cup unsweetened dairy-free milk of choice

1 tbsp maple syrup, 1–2 dates or sweetener of choice (optional)

¼ tsp vanilla extract (optional)

ice cubes, to serve (optional)

Place all the ingredients in a blender and blend until smooth. Adjust the consistency by adding some ice if it is too thin or more liquid if it is too thick.

HOT CHOCOLATE

Warm up this winter with a decadent cup of steaming hot chocolate. Top with dairy-free Whipped Cream (*see* page 82) or marshmallows.

Serves 2

2 tbsp cocoa powder

2 tbsp granulated sugar

500 ml/18 fl oz/2 cups unsweetened dairy-free milk, such as a combination of almond and coconut

3 tbsp dairy-free dark chocolate chips or 40 g/1½ oz chopped dark chocolate

½ tsp vanilla extract

dash ground nutmeg

Whisk the cocoa powder and sugar together in a saucepan. Slowly whisk in the milk until well blended with no lumps.

Heat over a medium-high heat, whisking frequently, until steaming. Add the chocolate and whisk until it is melted and combined. Remove from the heat and stir in the vanilla extract and nutmeg. Pour into mugs to serve.

BREAKFASTS

OVERNIGHT OATS WITH STRAWBERRIES

Whip up a batch of overnight oats and breakfast will be ready to go in the morning. I usually double this for my family, as it keeps for up to four days in the refrigerator, making another batch mid-week.

Serves 2

250 ml/8 fl oz/1 cup unsweetened dairy-free milk of choice, such as hemp, almond or coconut

100 g/3½ oz/⅔ cup steel-cut oats

1 tbsp chia seeds

6 strawberries, chopped

2 tbsp honey, maple syrup or sweetener of choice

½ tsp vanilla extract

75 g/3 oz/½ cup strawberries, sliced, to serve

Combine the milk, oats, chia seeds, chopped strawberries, honey and vanilla extract. Divide into two small Kilner or Mason jars. Cover and chill overnight.

When ready to serve, stir the oats. Eat chilled or heated through topped with sliced strawberries.

CLASSIC PORRIDGE
with Caramelized Pears & Nuts

Pinhead (steel-cut) oats topped with roasted sweet pears and toasted pecans are a hearty, healthy way to start your day. A delicious take on traditional porridge (oatmeal).

Serves 2

For the pears

2 ripe pears, sliced in half and cores removed

1 tbsp honey or maple syrup

1 tsp lemon juice

1 tbsp coconut oil

⅛ tsp ground cinnamon

dash ground cardamom or nutmeg

To serve

3 tbsp toasted chopped pecans

honey or maple syrup (optional)

ground cinnamon, for dusting

For the porridge

150 g/5 oz/1 cup pinhead (steel-cut) oats

500 ml/18 fl oz/2 cups unsweetened dairy-free milk, such as almond

250 ml/8 fl oz/1 cup water

2 tbsp, or to taste, honey or maple syrup

½ tsp vanilla extract

To make the pears, preheat the oven to 190°C/375°F/Gas Mark 5. Place the pear halves, cut side up, in a small baking dish and drizzle with honey and lemon juice. Dot the pears with coconut oil and sprinkle with cinnamon and cardamom. Bake for 20 minutes until softened, basting occasionally during baking with the pear juices in the dish.

Meanwhile, mix the oats, milk, water and honey together in a saucepan and cook over a medium-low heat, stirring frequently, until the oats are soft and creamy and the porridge has thickened. Stir in the vanilla. Divide the porridge between two bowls, then top each bowl with two pear halves and roasting juices. Top with pecans, honey or syrup, and cinnamon.

FRENCH TOAST STICKS
with Maple Syrup

Sweet cinnamon French toast sticks are a fun way to spice things up for breakfast.
Double the recipe and keep a few on hand in the freezer for a quick heat-and-go breakfast.

Serves 4

For the French toast sticks

3 medium (large) eggs

100 ml/3½ fl oz/⅓ cup unsweetened dairy-free milk,
    such as coconut or almond

2 tbsp granulated sugar or maple syrup

½ tsp vanilla extract

¼ tsp ground cinnamon

4 slices day-old, dairy-free bread

oil, for frying

To serve

icing (confectioners')
    sugar, for dusting

maple syrup

mixed berries of choice

Whisk the eggs, milk, sugar, vanilla extract and cinnamon together in a bowl. Pour into
a flat-bottomed baking dish for dipping the bread pieces.

Cut the bread slices into 4 portions, creating sticks.

Heat a frying pan over a medium heat, then oil the pan, and when the oil is hot, dip
each stick into the egg mixture and add to the pan. Cook the sticks until they are
golden brown on each side.

Dust with icing (confectioners') sugar and serve with maple syrup and berries.

HEARTY OAT MUFFINS

Add your favourite flavours to this hearty muffin. Fold in 100 g/3½ oz/¾ cup blueberries, toasted nuts, diced pear or whatever you enjoy to make them your own.

Makes 10 muffins

50 g/2 oz/¼ cup coconut oil or 100 ml/3½ fl oz/⅓ cup light-flavoured olive oil, plus
   extra for oiling (optional)

175 g/6 oz/1½ cups oat flour

100 g/3½ oz/1 cup rolled oats, plus extra for topping

½ tbsp baking powder

½ tbsp ground cinnamon

1 tsp bicarbonate of soda (baking soda)

½ tsp salt

250 ml/8 fl oz/1 cup unsweetened dairy-free milk of choice

2 medium (large) eggs

125 g/4 oz/⅓ cup honey or maple syrup

1 tsp vanilla extract

Preheat the oven to 180°C/350°F/Gas Mark 4. Oil a muffin tin or line with paper cases (baking cups). Set aside. Combine the oat flour, oats, baking powder, cinnamon, bicarbonate of soda (baking soda) and salt together in a bowl.

Whisk the milk, eggs, honey, coconut oil and vanilla together in another bowl.

Pour the wet mixture into the dry ingredients and mix together until just combined. Divide the batter evenly among the muffin holes in the tin or the cases, then sprinkle the batter with a few of the extra oats. Bake for 14–16 minutes until a toothpick poked into the centre of a muffin comes out clean. Allow to cool on a wire rack.

EGG MUFFINS WITH CHIVES & TOMATO

All the delicious flavours of an omelette, egg muffins come together in a flash for a protein-packed start to your day.

Serves 6

oil, for coating
8 medium (large) eggs
120 ml/4 fl oz/½ cup unsweetened dairy-free milk
salt and freshly ground black pepper
130 g/4½ oz/¾ cup diced tomatoes, deseeded
3 tbsp very finely chopped chives

Preheat the oven to 180°C/350°F/Gas Mark 4. Oil 6 holes of a muffin tin.

Whisk the eggs and milk together in a bowl until very well blended. Season with salt and pepper.

Stir in the tomatoes and chives, then divide the egg mixture among the 6 oiled holes of the muffin tin.

Bake for 15–20 minutes until the egg is set and cooked through.

BAKED AVOCADO EGG BOATS

These baked avocado egg boats are a breakfast recipe that will become an instant favourite. They also make a great lunch or light supper when served with a salad and fruit.

Serves 2

1 avocado, halved and pitted
2 medium (large) eggs
salt and freshly ground black pepper

To serve

1 tbsp cooked crumbled bacon
1 tsp very finely chopped chives

Preheat the oven to 220°C/425°F/Gas Mark 7.

If the cavity of the avocado is smaller than the egg, scoop out the cavity with a spoon to widen.

Place each avocado half into separate ramekins, flat side up. Crack an egg into the cavity in each avocado half and season with salt and pepper.

Bake for 12–15 minutes until the egg is cooked through. Remove from the oven and sprinkle with bacon and chives.

OAT & CARROT BREAKFAST BARS

Perfect for breakfast or as a healthy snack, these breakfast bars are packed with seeds for on-the-go protein.

Serves 8

6 tbsp water

2 tbsp chia seeds

oil, for oiling

100 g/3½ oz/1 cup finely ground almond flour or ground almonds

1 tsp ground cinnamon

½ tsp ground ginger

¼ tsp ground nutmeg

¼ tsp ground allspice

¼ tsp ground cardamom

¼ tsp salt

100 g/3½ oz/1 cup rolled oats

25 g/1 oz/½ cup unsweetened coconut flakes

200 g/7 oz/1½ cups finely grated carrots

250 g/9 oz/1 cup apple purée (applesauce)

75 g/3 oz/¼ cup honey

1 tsp vanilla extract

75 g/3 oz/½ cup sunflower seeds

75 g/3 oz/½ cup pumpkin seeds

For the topping

2 tbsp roasted salted sunflower seeds

3 tbsp roasted salted pumpkin seeds

Mix the water and chia seeds together in a bowl and set aside for 10 minutes, or until the chia seeds rehydrate and gel.

Preheat the oven to 180°C/350°F/Gas Mark 4. Oil a 23 x 33 cm/9 x 13 inch baking tin (pan) and line with baking parchment or foil and oil, leaving the edges overhanging the sides of the tin. Set aside.

Whisk the almond flour, spices and salt together in a bowl until well combined. Stir in the oats and coconut flakes.

Whisk the grated carrots, chia mixture, apple purée (applesauce), honey and vanilla extract together in another bowl.

Pour the carrot mixture into the oat mixture, add the sunflower seeds and pumpkin seeds and mix everything together until well blended.

Scoop the batter into the prepared tin and level the surface. Sprinkle the top with the roasted salted sunflower and pumpkin seeds and bake for 35–40 minutes until a toothpick inserted into the centre comes out clean.

Allow to cool on a wire rack before slicing.

EGGS BENEDICT

Eggs Benedict is also great made with bacon, Canadian bacon, thinly sliced smoked turkey or smoked salmon in place of the ham. Serve with a side of asparagus or roasted Brussels sprouts.

Serves 2 or 4, depending on how hungry you are!

For the hollandaise sauce

2 tsp white or rice vinegar

3 egg yolks

1 tbsp lemon juice

½ tsp salt, or to taste

4½ tbsp coconut oil, heated to about 32°C/90°F

⅛ tsp ground sweet paprika or dash cayenne pepper

For the eggs benedict

4 medium (large) eggs, as fresh as possible

2 English muffins, halved

225 g/8 oz shaved smoked ham

Buttery Spread (see page 78), for spreading (optional)

very finely chopped chives, to garnish

First, make the hollandaise sauce. Fill a saucepan two-thirds full with water and bring to the boil. Add the vinegar.

Pour the boiling water into a blender. Cover and leave for 5 minutes to heat the blender, then pour the water out and dry the blender.

Add the egg yolks, lemon juice and salt to the blender and process for 30 seconds on medium speed until the egg lightens in colour.

Turn the blender to its lowest setting, then while the machine is still running, slowly drizzle in the hot coconut oil. Turn the blender off, taste and adjust the salt, if necessary. Add the paprika and blend until just combined. Keep warm until ready to serve.

To poach the eggs, reduce the heat to a low simmer. Working with one egg at a time, crack an egg into a small bowl. Using the bowl, carefully slide the egg into the barely simmering water. Once it begins to solidify, slide in another egg, until all the eggs are in the pan. Turn off the heat and cover. Leave the eggs for 4–5 minutes, then gently lift them out with a slotted spoon. The timing will depend on how you like your eggs.

While the eggs are poaching, toast the English muffins, spread with the Buttery Spread, if using, and heat the ham. Set the muffin halves on serving plates and divide the ham between the muffins. Top the ham with an egg, then drizzle some hollandaise all over. Sprinkle with the chives.

INDULGENT BREAKFAST PANCAKES

Fluffy pancakes made without dairy are possible when you make your own dairy-free buttermilk replacement. Serve topped as shown in the recipe or with sautéed apples, fresh berries or simply with maple syrup or a drizzle of honey.

Serves 4

For the dairy-free buttermilk

350 ml/12 fl oz/1½ cups unsweetened dairy-free milk of choice, such as almond

1½ tsp cider vinegar, rice wine vinegar or lemon juice

For the pancakes

350 g/12 oz/2½ cups plus 2 tbsp plain (all-purpose) flour

1½ tsp baking powder

1½ tsp bicarbonate of soda (baking soda)

¼ tsp salt

3 medium (large) eggs

3 tbsp maple syrup

1½ tsp vanilla extract

½ tsp ground cinnamon (optional)

oil, for cooking

For the toppings

Buttery Spread (*see* page 78), optional

sliced bananas

toasted chopped hazelnuts

maple syrup

To make the buttermilk, whisk the milk and vinegar together. Set aside for 5 minutes.

For the pancakes, whisk the flour, baking powder, bicarbonate of soda (baking soda) and salt together. Add the buttermilk, eggs, maple syrup, vanilla and cinnamon and stir until the batter is just combined. Allow to stand for 10 minutes.

Heat a small amount of oil in a frying pan over a medium heat. Pour 3–4 tbsp batter per pancake into the pan and cook until the pancake is bubbly and set around the edge. Flip over with a spatula and cook on the other side until golden brown and cooked through.

If you would like to serve the pancakes all at once, place the cooked pancakes on a baking sheet in a 93°C/200°F/Gas Mark ¼ oven to keep warm until serving.

Top the pancakes with Buttery Spread, sliced bananas, toasted chopped hazelnuts and maple syrup.

SNACKS, SIDES & SMALL DISHES

CHEESY CRACKERS

Dairy-free crackers that are crisp and crunchy with a bold cheese flavour.

Serves 4-6

125 g/4 oz/1 cup plain (all-purpose) flour, plus extra for dusting

2 tbsp nutritional yeast flakes

1 tsp salt

¼ tsp onion powder

⅛ tsp ground turmeric

¼ tsp baking powder

5 tbsp cold dairy-free Buttery Spread (*see* page 78) or cold white vegetable fat (shortening) or 3½ tbsp cold coconut oil

3 tbsp cold water

Pulse the flour, nutritional yeast, salt, onion powder, turmeric and baking powder in a food processor until combined. Add the Buttery Spread and pulse until the mixture looks crumbly. Add the water, 1 tbsp at a time, and pulse just until the dough comes together. Flatten the dough into a disc and wrap in plastic wrap. Chill.

When ready to bake, preheat the oven to 190°C/375°F/Gas Mark 5 and line a baking sheet with baking parchment.Working with half the dough at a time, roll the dough out on a lightly floured work surface until it is about 3 mm/⅛ inch thick. Cut the dough into equal-size squares, approximately 2 cm/¾ inch, with a knife or pizza cutter and pierce each square in the centre with a straw or skewer.

Place the squares 1 cm/½ inch apart on the prepared baking sheet. Bake for 12–15 minutes until golden. Transfer to a wire rack to cool. Store at room temperature in a tightly sealed container.

AVOCADO CHEESE TOASTIE

The ultimate in comfort food isn't out of reach when you use one of the dairy-free cheeses, such as Cashew Nut Cheese (*see* page 61), to make this indulgent toastie (grilled cheese sandwich). Can't have nuts? Use the nut-free stretchy spread instead.

Serves 2

olive oil, coconut oil or dairy-free Buttery Spread (*see* page 78)

4 slices bread

4 slices dairy-free cheese of choice or stretchy nut-free option below

1 avocado, halved, pitted, peeled and sliced

15 g/½ oz/½ cup baby spinach leaves or basil leaves

Spread the oil or Buttery Spread on one side of each bread slice. Turn the oiled sides of bread face down and top two of them with a cheese slice (or spread). (The oiled sides of the bread will be on the outside of the sandwiches.) Put the avocado and spinach on top of the cheese and then add another layer of cheese, before placing a bread slice on each, with the oiled side of the bread on the outside.

Heat a medium frying pan over a medium-low heat. Carefully place the sandwiches in the heated pan, cover and cook for 3–5 minutes until golden brown. Flip and cook the other side until golden brown and the cheese has melted. Serve immediately.

Nut-free Stretchy Cheese Spread

Whisk 10 g/¼ oz/¼ cup nutritional yeast flakes, 2 tbsp tapioca flour (starch), ½ tsp salt, ¼ tsp garlic powder and 250 ml/8 fl oz/1 cup water together in a pan. Cook over a medium heat, whisking constantly until it thickens and bubbles. Cook for 30 seconds more, then remove from the heat. Whisk in 2 tbsp Buttery Spread or oil and ½ tsp mustard until combined. It will thicken as it cools. Cover and chill until needed.

QUICHE LORRAINE

Quiche makes a lovely brunch dish or the centrepiece to a light lunch served with a salad and fruit. Probably the most famous quiche, Quiche Lorraine is named for its region of origin. The classic recipe contains no cheese, so feel free to skip the dairy-free cheese and increase the ham and onion, if you like.

Serves 6

For the crust

125 g/4 oz/1 cup plain (all-purpose) flour or favourite flour blend,
   plus extra for dusting

¼ tsp salt

65 g/2½ oz/⅓ cup cold lard or white vegetable fat (shortening)

3–4 tbsp cold water

For the quiche

65 g/2½ oz/½ cup chopped ham or cooked crumbled bacon

½ small onion, chopped

125 g/4 oz/1 cup grated dairy-free Swiss Cheese (see page 74)

4 medium (large) eggs

250 ml/8 fl oz/1 cup unsweetened mild-flavoured dairy-free milk, such as almond

225 g/8 oz/1 cup canned full-fat coconut milk

½ tsp salt

¼ tsp freshly ground black pepper

⅛ tsp ground nutmeg

For the crust, combine the flour and salt together in a bowl. Using two forks or a pastry blender, cut in the lard until the mixture looks like coarse crumbs without any piece of lard larger than a small pea. Drizzle the flour mixture with water, 1 tbsp at a time, tossing with a fork between additions, until the mixture comes together and holds when pressed. Shape the dough into a ball and flatten slightly. Wrap in plastic wrap and chill until ready to use.

To assemble the quiche, roll out the dough on a lightly floured work surface to 5 mm/¼ inch thick. Press the dough onto the bottom and up the sides of a quiche tin (pan), then trim the dough flush with the top edge of the tin. Prick the bottom all over with a fork. Transfer the tin to a rimmed baking sheet and freeze while the oven is preheating.

Preheat the oven to 190°C/375°F/Gas Mark 5.

When the oven has reached the correct temperature, remove the crust from the freezer. Sprinkle the ham and onion over the crust, then top with the cheese.

Whisk the eggs, both milks, salt, pepper and nutmeg together in a bowl until well incorporated. Pour the mixture into the crust.

Place the quiche in the oven, reduce the oven temperature to 160°C/325°F/Gas Mark 3 and bake for 40–45 minutes until the filling has set. Allow to cool for 10 minutes before serving.

CORN, BACON & PRAWN CHOWDER

Rich corn chowder gets get bold kick of flavour from the prawns (shrimp) and bacon. Loaded with sweetcorn, crisp bacon and meaty prawns, this chowder makes a weeknight dinner into an event.

Serves 6

5 rashers (slices) thick-cut bacon, cut into 1 cm/½ inch pieces

1 tbsp olive oil

4 salad (green) onions, thinly sliced, green and white parts separated

165 g/5½ oz/1 cup fresh or frozen sweetcorn, very finely chopped, saving all juice and pulp

1 large stick celery, diced

4 garlic cloves, peeled and very finely chopped or 6 roasted garlic cloves, peeled and very finely chopped

2 tbsp plain (all-purpose) flour or 1 tbsp cornflour (cornstarch)

½ tsp salt, or to taste

¼ tsp freshly ground black pepper, or to taste

600 ml/1 pint/2½ cups unsweetened creamy dairy-free milk of choice, such as almond

225 g/8 oz/1½ cups fresh or frozen sweetcorn

¼ tsp cayenne pepper, or to taste

450 g/1 lb thawed prawns (shrimp), peeled, deveined and tails removed

100 ml/3½ fl oz/⅓ cup canned coconut milk, not low fat

½ tsp dried thyme or ½ tbsp thyme leaves

hot sauce, to serve (optional)

Cook the bacon in a soup pot or casserole dish (Dutch oven) until crisp. Remove and set aside for serving. Drain all but 1–2 tbsp melted bacon fat.

Add the oil to the pot. Set aside 20 g/¾ oz/¼ cup of the sliced salad (green) onions for serving, then add the remaining onions, the sweetcorn and celery and cook, stirring frequently, for about 3 minutes until the vegetables are tender. Add the garlic and stir, cooking for 30 seconds, or until the garlic is fragrant.

Sprinkle the flour, salt and pepper over the vegetables and cook, stirring constantly, for 1 minute. Slowly pour in the unsweetened milk, whisking while it is being added. Add the remaining sweetcorn and cayenne pepper. Stir and bring to a simmer, stirring frequently. Continue to stir frequently, simmering for 5 minutes, or until the mixture thickens. Be careful not to let the mixture scorch.

Stir in the prawns (shrimp) and cook for 5 minutes, or until the prawns are cooked through. Remove from the heat and stir in the coconut milk and thyme. Stir well.

To serve, pour into bowls and sprinkle with reserved bacon and salad onions and a dash of hot sauce, if liked.

CHEESY BROCCOLI SOUP

This delicious soup is loaded with tender broccoli, comforting potatoes and cheesy goodness, while still being dairy free.

Serves 6

575 g/1¼ lb golden potatoes, such as Yukon Gold

1 medium carrot, sliced

1 litre/1¾ pints/4 cups chicken or vegetable stock

10 g/¼ oz/¼ cup nutritional yeast flakes or 2 tbsp nutritional yeast powder

3½ tbsp olive oil

2 medium onions, chopped

2 garlic cloves, peeled and very finely chopped

¾ tsp dried oregano

½ tsp dried thyme

100 g/3½ oz/1½ cups frozen broccoli florets, thawed, or steamed fresh broccoli, cut into small pieces

⅛ tsp ground nutmeg

salt and freshly ground black pepper

To make the soup cheese base, place 100 g/3½ oz/1 cup of the potatoes and the carrots in a saucepan, cover with water and bring to the boil. Cook until the vegetables are tender. Drain and put the vegetables into a blender with 120 ml/4 fl oz/½ cup of the stock, the nutritional yeast and 1½ tbsp olive oil and blend until very smooth. Set aside.

To make the soup, heat the remaining oil in a soup pot over a medium-high heat, add the onion and fry until translucent. Add the garlic, oregano and thyme and fry for another minute. Add 500 ml/18 fl oz/2 cups stock and the remaining potatoes. Bring to the boil, then reduce to a simmer and cook until the potatoes are tender. Mash the potatoes coarsely in the pot with a potato masher or fork, keeping the texture and pieces of potato to enjoy in the soup. Pour the finished soup cheese base into the pot. Add the broccoli, nutmeg and 250 ml/8 fl oz/1 cup stock. Stir and heat through. Check the seasoning and soup thickness to see if you need to add the remaining stock or additional salt and pepper before serving.

CRISPY KALE SNACK

Kale is one of the healthiest vegetables you can eat, but that doesn't mean you can't have fun with it. This satisfies the need for a crunchy salty snack while having something still packed with fibre, calcium and vitamins K, C and A.

Serves 4

1 large bunch kale, stems removed
2 tbsp olive oil
2 tbsp lemon juice
½ tsp salt, or to taste

Preheat the oven to 180°C/350°F/Gas Mark 4. Line two rimmed baking sheets with baking parchment. Set aside.

Tear or cut the kale into approximately 5–7.5 cm/2–3 inch pieces. Place the kale in a large bowl and drizzle with olive oil and lemon juice. Sprinkle with salt and massage the toppings into the kale leaves, distributing the topping evenly.

Put the kale on the prepared baking sheets and bake for 10–15 minutes until crispy. Turn the baking sheets halfway through baking. Cool and serve.

CRANBERRY NUT CHEESE BALLS

These cheese balls are a fun starter (appetizer) to serve during the holidays or on special occasions. They can be made up to two days before you need to serve them.

Serves 4

For the cream cheese

350 ml/12 fl oz/1½ cups plain dairy-free yogurt, or 175 g/6 oz bought dairy-free cream cheese

For the cheese ball base

1 quantity Goat's Cheese (*see* page 70)

2 tsp ground cinnamon

3 tbsp honey

¼ tsp freshly ground black pepper

25 g/1 oz/¼ cup toasted pecans, finely chopped

25 g/1 oz/¼ cup very finely chopped dried cranberries

To coat

125 g/4 oz/1 cup toasted pecans, finely chopped

125 g/4 oz/1 cup dried cranberries, finely chopped

15 g/½ oz/½ cup very finely chopped parsley

If making the cream cheese, put the yogurt in a sieve (strainer) lined with butter muslin (cheesecloth). Set the sieve in a bowl. Cover and chill overnight. The next day, the yogurt will have drained and thickened. Drain until it is the texture of cream cheese.

To make the cheese ball base, mix the cream cheese, Goat's Cheese, cinnamon, honey and black pepper together in a bowl until completely blended. Stir in the pecans and cranberries, then cover and chill.

To make the balls, using a spoon such as a coffee scoop, scoop balls of the chilled cheese mixture, then with lightly dampened hands, roll into smooth balls. To coat, mix the pecans, cranberries and parsley together on a rimmed plate and roll the balls in the mixture until completely coated. Store in an airtight container and chill until ready to serve.

CHICKEN & MANGO SALAD
with Green Goddess Dressing

The combination of chicken, mango and watercress is the perfect palette for zesty green goddess dressing.

Serves 4

2 x 175 g/6 oz cooked chicken breasts, thinly sliced

2 mangoes, peeled, pitted and chopped

2 bunches watercress, thick stems removed, cleaned

10 g/¼ oz/⅓ cup mint, stems removed, torn or chopped

2 salad (green) onions, green and white parts thinly sliced

65 g/2½ oz/½ cup walnuts, chopped

freshly cracked black pepper (optional)

For the dressing

50 g/2 oz/2 cups parsley, chopped

10 g/¼ oz/½ cup basil leaves or dill

4 salad (green) onions, green and white parts chopped

150 g/5 oz/⅔ cup dairy-free mayonnaise

50 ml/2 fl oz/¼ cup dairy-free yogurt

1 tbsp lemon juice

½ tbsp very finely chopped lemon zest

½ garlic clove, peeled and very finely chopped

1 tsp salt, or to taste

½ tsp ground black pepper

1 tsp anchovy paste, or 1–2 anchovy fillets (optional)

Put all the dressing ingredients into a food processor or blender and pulse until the herbs are all very finely chopped and the dip is creamy, scraping down the sides of the food processor as needed. Cover and chill until ready to serve.

Divide the chicken among four plates and set aside.

Toss the mangoes, watercress, mint and salad (green) onions together in a bowl. Divide the mixture among the four plates on top of the chicken.

Drizzle the dressing over the top and add the walnuts. Season with cracked black pepper, if liked.

CHEESY POTATO WEDGES

Soaking the potato wedges in iced water before cooking seems like an unusual extra step. However, doing so removes excess potato starch, preventing the wedges from sticking together, and helps them become even crispier. If needed for later in the day, the wedges can be stored in the iced water in the refrigerator for several hours.

Serves 4-6

4 baking potatoes, such as Russet,
    cut into similar-size wedges
16 ice cubes (2 cups)
3–4 tbsp olive oil
½ tsp paprika
¼ tsp garlic powder
¼ tsp dried rosemary

¼ tsp salt, or to taste
¼ tsp freshly ground black pepper,
    or to taste
25 g/1 oz/¼ cup finely grated Cashew
    Nut Cheese (*see* page 61) or dairy-
    free Parmesan (*see* page 73)
2 tbsp very finely chopped parsley

Preheat the oven to 230°C/450°F/Gas Mark 8. Line a rimmed baking sheet with baking parchment or foil. Set aside. Place the potatoes in a bowl of cold water with the ice cubes and allow to stand for 30 minutes. Drain and pat dry, then place the wedges in a bowl.

Whisk 3 tbsp olive oil, paprika, garlic powder, rosemary, salt and pepper together in a bowl. Pour over the potato wedges and toss to coat the potatoes evenly, adding another 1 tbsp olive oil if needed to completely coat the wedges. Place the seasoned potatoes on the prepared baking sheet in a single layer and bake for 30–40 minutes, tossing every 15–20 minutes during baking until the potatoes are tender and cooked through on the inside, crisp and golden brown on the outside.

Meanwhile, mix the cheese and parsley together. When the potatoes have finished baking, sprinkle with the cheese mixture and serve immediately.

GARLIC SPINACH POTATO GRATIN

Served with roast turkey or beef, this potato gratin makes any dinner special. Savoury shallots, spinach and tender potatoes are enrobed with a rich garlic-infused sauce and baked to a crispy finish.

Serves 6–8

For the roasted garlic

1 whole garlic bulb
2 tsp olive oil

For the gratin

2 tbsp olive oil
3 shallots, thinly sliced
225 g/8 oz fresh spinach, chopped
1 quantity dairy-free Béchamel Sauce
   (*see* page 90)

¼ tsp ground nutmeg
700 g/1½ lb golden potatoes, such as
   Yukon Gold, very thinly sliced
100 g/3½ oz/1 cup grated dairy-free
   cheese, such as Cashew Nut (*see*
   page 61) or dairy-free Mozzarella
   (*see* page 68)
25 g/1 oz/⅓ cup grated dairy-free
   Parmesan (*see* page 73)
ground paprika, for dusting (optional)

To roast the garlic, preheat the oven to 180°C/350°F/Gas Mark 4. Slice a thin layer off the top of the garlic bulb to expose the cloves inside. Set the garlic on a piece of foil. Drizzle with olive oil and close up the foil, completely encasing the garlic. Place on a baking sheet and bake for 35 minutes, or until the garlic is very tender. Allow to cool until it can be handled safely, then squeeze out the roasted garlic into a small bowl. Set aside. Keep the oven on. Grease a 2.8 litre/5 pint/3 quart baking dish and set aside.

Heat the olive oil in a frying pan over a medium-high heat, add the shallots and fry until translucent. Add the spinach and cook, stirring, until the spinach has wilted. Add the roasted garlic, stir and remove from the heat. Stir the spinach mixture into the Béchamel Sauce in a bowl, then stir in the nutmeg.

Put the potatoes into the bowl with the béchamel mixture and stir until the potatoes are coated with the sauce. Place one third of the potato mixture on the bottom of the prepared dish in an even layer. Top with half the grated cheese, then add another one third of the potato mixture, then the rest of the cheese, finishing with the last third of the potato mixture. Pour any remaining sauce over the potatoes and level the surface. Sprinkle with Parmesan and paprika, if using.

Cover the dish with foil and bake for 1 hour. Uncover and bake for another 15–20 minutes until the potatoes are tender and the top is golden brown.

COMFORTING MAINS

HOMELY FISH PIE

Perfect for autumn (fall) or spring, this fish pie is a wonderful comforting dish, yet not too heavy if the weather is not very chilly. Use only salmon as listed, or choose any firm fish or combination of fish and shellfish to make this dish. I like a combination of cod and prawns (shrimp).

Serves 4-6

1 tbsp olive oil, plus extra for oiling

900 g/2 lb potatoes, peeled and quartered

4 tbsp unsweetened mild-flavoured dairy-free milk of choice, such as almond

2 tbsp Buttery Spread (*see* page 78) or coconut or olive oil

salt and freshly ground black pepper

50 g/2 oz/½ cup chopped asparagus

75 g/3 oz/½ cup fresh or frozen peas

4 salad (green) onions, green and white parts thinly sliced

1 quantity dairy-free Béchamel Sauce (*see* page 90)

65 g/2½ oz/½ cup grated dairy-free Mozzarella (*see* page 68) or Cashew Nut
   Cheese (*see* page 61)

1 tsp dried tarragon or thyme

900 g/2 lb salmon fillets, cooked and skin removed

Preheat the oven to 180°C/350°F/Gas Mark 4. Oil a large baking dish and set aside.

Put the potatoes in a large saucepan and cover with water. Cover with the lid and bring to the boil. Reduce the heat and simmer for 10–15 minutes until the potatoes are tender. Drain and mash with the milk and Buttery Spread. Season to taste with salt and pepper.

Heat the olive oil in a frying pan over a medium heat, add the asparagus, peas and salad (green) onions and fry until the asparagus is tender. Stir the vegetables into the Béchamel Sauce in a bowl, add the grated cheese, tarragon and salt and pepper to taste.

Break the cooked salmon up into the bottom of the prepared baking dish. Pour the béchamel and vegetable mixture over and gently stir to distribute the sauce and vegetables evenly around the salmon. Put the mashed potatoes into a decorating bag with a large star tip and carefully pipe stars of mashed potatoes on top of the sauce. The stars should be touching to completely cover the surface of the sauce. Alternatively, dollop the warm mashed potatoes over the sauce and carefully spread to cover. Bake for 20–25 minutes until the mixture is bubbling and the potatoes are golden.

CREAMY CHICKEN
with Sun-dried Tomatoes

Succulent chicken baked to perfection with a savoury sauce of sun-dried tomatoes and fresh herbs. Serve with roasted squash or oven-roasted Brussels sprouts or potatoes.

Serves 8

8 bone-in chicken thighs or 4 chicken legs

salt and freshly ground black pepper

2 tbsp olive oil

3 garlic cloves, peeled and very
   finely chopped

250 ml/8 fl oz/1 cup chicken stock

½ tsp dried thyme

½ tsp dried oregano

¼ tsp dried red chilli (red pepper) flakes

120 ml/4 fl oz/½ cup canned coconut
   milk, not low fat

40 g/1½ oz/⅓ cup chopped sun-dried
   tomatoes

25 g/1 oz/¼ cup grated dairy-free
   Parmesan (*see* page 73)

10 g/¼ oz/¼ cup basil, torn or thinly sliced

2–3 cherry tomatoes, to garnish
   (optional)

Preheat the oven to 200°C/400°F/Gas Mark 6. Season the chicken with salt and pepper. Heat the oil in a frying pan over a medium-high heat, add the chicken and sear on both sides for 2–3 minutes until golden brown. Place in a large ovenproof baking dish.

Add the garlic to the hot oil and fry, stirring, for 1 minute. Add the stock, thyme, oregano and chilli (red pepper) flakes and scrape the browned bits from the bottom of the pan as the stock is heating. When the stock is warm, add the coconut milk, sun-dried tomatoes and Parmesan. Bring to a gentle boil, stirring frequently, then reduce the heat and simmer for 3–5 minutes until the sauce is slightly thickened. Pour the sauce over the chicken and bake for 25–30 minutes until the chicken is cooked through. Serve sprinkled with torn basil leaves and a few cut cherry tomatoes, if liked.

BEEF STEW WITH DUMPLINGS

On blustery winter evenings, nothing warms you up quite like a rich beef stew topped with fluffy dumplings.

Serves 4

2–3 tbsp olive oil

450 g/1 lb stewing beef, cut into bite-size pieces

2 tbsp plain (all-purpose) flour or 1 tbsp cornflour (cornstarch)

3 garlic cloves, peeled and very finely chopped

2 leeks, chopped

1½ onions, peeled and chopped

1½ sticks celery, chopped

1½ carrots, peeled and chopped

200 g/7 oz/1½ cups swede (rutabaga), turnip, parsnip, potato or a mixture, chopped

100 ml/3½ fl oz/⅓ cup red wine or beef stock

325 ml/11¼ fl oz/1⅓ cups beef stock

1 tbsp dried thyme or 3 tbsp thyme leaves

1–2 tbsp, or to taste Worcestershire sauce

1 tbsp balsamic vinegar, or to taste

2 bay leaves

salt and freshly ground black pepper

3 tbsp chopped parsley (optional)

For the dumplings

125 g/4 oz/1 cup plain (all-purpose) flour, plus extra for dusting

1 tsp baking powder

¼ tsp salt

65 g/2½ oz/⅓ cup cold lard or white vegetable fat (shortening), cut into chunks

Preheat the oven to 180°C/350°F/Gas Mark 4. Heat the oil in an ovenproof casserole dish (Dutch oven) over a medium-high heat, add the beef and brown on each side. Sprinkle over the flour and cook for another 3 minutes. Add the garlic and vegetables to the beef and cook for 2–3 minutes, stirring occasionally. Stir in the wine, stock, thyme, Worcestershire sauce, vinegar and bay leaves and season with salt and pepper. Cover with a lid and cook in the oven for 2 hours, or until cooked through and tender.

For the dumplings, pulse the flour, baking powder and salt together in a food processor. Add the lard or white vegetable fat (shortening) and pulse until the lard is the size of small peas. Add cold water, 1–2 tbsp at a time, and pulse until a thick dough forms. Break off spoonfuls of the dough and lightly roll into balls with floured hands.

After the stew has cooked for 2 hours, remove from the oven and place the dumplings on top of the stew. Cover and bake for another 20 minutes until the dumplings are cooked through. If you like dumplings that are golden, remove the lid halfway through the final cooking. Garnish with parsley, if liked.

BAKED MAC & CHEESE

I often simply stir my dairy-free cashew-based cheese sauce into cooked pasta to make mac and cheese, but what to do when you want a creamy nut-free dish? This is the ultimate cheesy baked mac and cheese, made without a single nut.

Serves 4-6

oil, for oiling

400 g/14 oz packet macaroni

2 slices bread

1½ tbsp Buttery Spread (*see* page 78), coconut or olive oil

For the sauce

450 g/1 lb/2 cups cooked and mashed white or yellow sweet potato or yam

75 g/3 oz/¾ cup cauliflower florets, cooked and cooled

100 g/3½ oz/⅓ cup white miso paste

1½ tsp salt, or to taste

1 tsp prepared mustard

20 g/¾ oz/½ cup nutritional yeast flakes, or 10 g/¼ oz/¼ cup nutritional yeast powder

1 tbsp tapioca flour (starch)

250 ml/8 fl oz/1 cup unsweetened mild-flavoured dairy-free milk

1 tbsp cider vinegar

¼ tsp garlic powder

¼ tsp onion powder

⅛ tsp ground turmeric

⅛ tsp ground paprika

1 tbsp Buttery Spread, coconut or olive oil (optional)

Preheat the oven to 190°C/375°F/Gas Mark 5. Oil a large baking dish and set aside. Fill a large saucepan with water and bring to the boil. Add the macaroni and cook according to the packet instructions until tender. Drain, rinse, then return to the pan.

Meanwhile, put all the sauce ingredients into a high-powered blender and blend until very smooth. Pour into a saucepan and heat, whisking frequently, until warm. Check the seasoning and adjust if necessary.

Pour over the cheese sauce over the cooked macaroni and stir gently to combine. Spoon into the prepared baking dish and level the surface.

Pulse the bread in a food processor or blender to make crumbs. Add the Buttery Spread and pulse until it is evenly combined with the crumbs. Sprinkle over the macaroni. Bake for 25–30 minutes until it is hot all the way through and the topping is golden brown.

YOGURT CHICKEN CURRY

A takeaway classic you can make at home. If you don't have any dairy-free yogurt to hand, mix 250 ml/8 fl oz/1 cup canned coconut milk and 1 tbsp cider vinegar and add to the marinade instead of the yogurt. Leftovers freeze and reheat well.

Serves 4

For the marinated chicken

800 g/1¾ lb skinless, boneless chicken thighs, trimmed and cut into pieces

250 ml/8 fl oz/1 cup unsweetened dairy-free yogurt, such as coconut

3 tbsp finely grated fresh root ginger or 1 tbsp ground ginger

1½ tbsp very finely chopped garlic

2 tsp garam masala

1 tsp ground turmeric

1 tsp ground cumin

1 tsp chilli powder

1 tsp salt

For the sauce

2 tbsp coconut or olive oil

2 tbsp Buttery Spread (*see* page 78), coconut or olive oil

1 large onion, diced

1½ tbsp very finely chopped garlic

1 tbsp finely grated fresh root ginger or 1 tsp ground ginger

1½ tsp garam masala

1½ tsp ground cumin

1 tsp ground turmeric

1 tsp ground coriander

400 g/14 oz can tomato sauce or purée (paste)

1 tsp paprika

1 tsp chilli powder (optional, depending on how spicy you like it)

1 tsp salt

300 ml/10 fl oz/1¼ cups canned full-fat coconut milk

1 tsp brown sugar or honey

50 ml/2 fl oz/¼ cup water or chicken stock (optional)

To serve

hot cooked rice

very finely chopped coriander (cilantro) or parsley

To marinate the chicken, mix the chicken, yogurt, ginger, garlic, spices and salt in a large bowl or resealable plastic bag. Cover the bowl or seal the bag and chill for at least 1 hour, or overnight.

To make the curry, heat the oil in a large frying pan over a medium-high heat. Working in three batches, when the oil is hot, add the chicken, making sure not to overcrowd the pan and cook for 3 minutes on each side until the chicken is browned. Transfer the chicken to a bowl and keep warm while you cook the remaining chicken.

In the same frying pan, add the Buttery Spread and, when hot, add the onion. Cook, stirring, until translucent. Add the garlic and ginger and fry for 1 minute. Add the garam masala, cumin, turmeric and coriander and fry for another minute until fragrant. Pour in the tomato sauce, paprika, chilli powder and salt, stir well and bring to a simmer. Cook, whisking frequently, for 10–15 minutes until the sauce thickens and has deepened in colour.

Stir the coconut milk and brown sugar into the tomato sauce. Add the chicken and any juices in the bowl, stir and cook for about 10 minutes until the chicken is cooked through and the sauce is bubbling. If the sauce becomes too thick, stir in a little water or chicken stock to thin.

Serve over rice and sprinkle with coriander (cilantro).

GOOD OL` LASAGNE

Traditional lasagne made dairy free. I often double the recipe and assemble two lasagnes at a time, one for dinner and one for another day. Wrap the second well and freeze. To serve, thaw overnight in the refrigerator and double the baking time.

Serves 6

For the meat sauce

oil, for oiling

450 g/1 lb lean minced (ground) beef, or half minced beef and half Italian sausage

4 garlic cloves, peeled and very finely chopped

½ tsp freshly ground black pepper

¼ tsp dried chilli (red pepper) flakes

720 ml/1¼ pints/3 cups bottled tomato sauce (marinara sauce)

For the ricotta layer

1 quantity dairy-free Ricotta (*see* page 67)

1 medium (large) egg

2 tbsp very finely chopped parsley

1 tbsp very finely chopped oregano leaves

1 tbsp olive oil or melted Buttery Spread (*see* page 78)

1 garlic clove, peeled and very finely chopped

To assemble

450 g/16 oz packet lasagne sheets (noodles),
   cooked according to packet instructions

1 quantity dairy-free Mozzarella (*see* page 68), grated,
   about 175 g/6 oz/1½ cups

25 g/1 oz/¼ cup grated dairy-free Parmesan (*see* page 73)

Preheat the oven to 190°C/375°F/Gas Mark 5. Oil a 28 x 18 cm/11 x 7 inch baking dish.

To make the sauce, cook the beef in a frying pan over a medium-high heat, breaking up the beef until browned and cooked through. Drain off any grease, if needed. Add the garlic, pepper and dried chilli (red pepper) flakes and cook for 1 minute, stirring. Pour the tomato (marinara) sauce over the cooked beef, stir well and remove from the heat.

To make the ricotta layer, combine the Ricotta, egg, parsley, oregano, oil and garlic together in a bowl. Set aside.

To assemble the lasagne, spread 120 ml/4 fl oz/½ cup meat sauce in the bottom of the prepared baking dish. Arrange a single layer of cooked lasagne sheets (noodles) on top, then spread another 250 ml/8 fl oz/1 cup meat sauce over evenly. Top with another layer of pasta sheets.

Stir 65 g/2½ oz/½ cup grated Mozzarella into the ricotta mixture, then dollop over the pasta, carefully spreading into an even layer. Top with a layer of pasta sheets.

Spread 250 ml/8 fl oz/1 cup meat sauce on top, then add a final layer of pasta. Pour the remaining sauce over the pasta, spreading evenly. Sprinkle with the remaining Mozzarella and the Parmesan.

Cover the dish with oiled foil and bake for 30 minutes. Uncover and bake for another 10–14 minutes until bubbling. Allow to stand for 10 minutes before serving.

PIZZA WITH PEPPER & `RICOTTA`

A quick pizza with sweet red peppers, fresh herbs and dairy-free ricotta to make a change from standard pizza fare. A great light supper or lunch, or fun to share at a party.

Serves 2–4

400–450 g/14–16 oz ball pizza dough, thawed and risen, or 33 cm/13 inch par-baked crust

50 ml/2 fl oz/¼ cup olive oil

3 garlic cloves, peeled and very finely chopped

1 tsp dried oregano

½ tsp crushed dried chilli (red pepper) flakes

15 g/½ oz/½ cup baby spinach leaves, chopped (optional)

¼–⅓ medium red onion, peeled and thinly sliced or 25 g/1 oz/¼ cup thinly sliced shallots

1 sweet red pepper, thinly sliced

250 g/9 oz/1 cup dairy-free Ricotta (see page 67) or dairy-free Goat's Cheese (see page 70), crumbled

2 tbsp very finely chopped basil leaves

1 tbsp very finely chopped oregano leaves

1 tbsp very finely chopped parsley

Preheat the oven to 200°C/400°F/Gas Mark 6. Pat out the pizza dough on a baking sheet into a 33 cm/13 inch round. Bake for 7–10 minutes until just set, but not golden.

Mix the olive oil, garlic, dried oregano and dried chilli (red pepper) flakes together. Brush over the par-baked pizza crust, then top with the spinach, if using. Sprinkle with red onions, peppers, then the Ricotta or Goat's Cheese.

Mix the fresh basil, oregano and parsley together in a small bowl. Sprinkle half on the pizza and drizzle with the remaining olive oil mixture. Return the pizza to the oven and bake for 10–15 minutes until golden. Sprinkle the pizza with the remaining fresh herbs before slicing.

BUTTERMILK ROAST CHICKEN

Dairy-free buttermilk helps to tenderize the chicken, while the flavours of the herbs infuse it, creating a moist, flavourful bird.

Serves 8

1.4–1.8 kg/3–4 lb whole chicken,
   cleaned, giblets removed
1 tsp salt
oil, for oiling
1 onion, peeled and quartered
several rosemary sprigs (optional)
several.thyme sprigs (optional)
1 tbsp Buttery Spread (*see* page 78),
   melted, or oil of choice
paprika, for sprinkling

For the buttermilk marinade

1 litre/1¾ pints/4 cups
   unsweetened creamy dairy-free
   milk of choice, such as coconut
   or almond
4 tsp cider vinegar
2 garlic cloves, peeled and
   crushed
2 tbsp rosemary leaves
1 tbsp thyme leaves

To make the buttermilk marinade, stir the milk and vinegar together and set aside for 10 minutes. Stir in the garlic, rosemary and thyme leaves.

For the chicken, place the chicken in a non-reactive bowl and sprinkle with the salt. Rub the salt into the skin. Pour over the buttermilk marinade and turn the chicken around until coated. Leave the chicken, breast side down, in the bowl and cover with plastic wrap. Chill for a minimum of 6 hours, or overnight.

When ready to bake, preheat the oven to 180°C/350°F/Gas Mark 4 and oil a roasting pan. Remove the chicken from the marinade and discard the liquid. Put the chicken into the prepared roasting pan and stuff the cavity of the chicken with onion wedges, rosemary and thyme sprigs.

Use kitchen string or butcher's twine to truss the chicken. Tuck the chicken wings under the chicken.

Bake for 20 minutes for each 450 g/1 lb, plus another 15 minutes until the chicken is cooked through. If the chicken browns too much before it is cooked, tent with foil. When there is 15 minutes left of baking time, remove any foil and brush the chicken with Buttery Spread or oil and sprinkle with paprika. The internal temperature will be 71°C/160°F in the thickest part when the chicken is cooked. Rest for 20 minutes before carving.

VEGETABLE COUSCOUS TAGINE

To make this recipe gluten free, simply replace the couscous with quinoa. Simmer for 15 minutes instead of turning off the heat. To add some protein, stir in 200 g/7 oz/1½ cups canned chickpeas when adding the couscous.

Serves 4

1½ tbsp olive oil

1¼ medium red onions, peeled and thinly sliced

1 tbsp very finely chopped garlic

1 tbsp grated fresh root ginger

2 small courgettes (zucchini), cut in half lengthways, then into 1 cm/½ inch slices

½ sweet red pepper, sliced

½ sweet yellow pepper, sliced

2 tsp ground cumin

1 tsp chilli powder

¼ tsp ground turmeric

salt and freshly ground black pepper

350 ml/12 fl oz/1½ cups vegetable or chicken stock

175 g/6 oz/1 cup uncooked couscous

100 g/3½ oz/¾ cup sultanas (golden raisins)

100 g/3½ oz/¾ cup sliced cherry tomatoes or chopped Roma tomatoes

5 g/⅛ oz/¼ cup chopped coriander (cilantro)

To serve

130 g/4½ oz/½ cup dairy-free Goat's Cheese (*see* page 70)

2 tbsp sliced salad (green) onions, green parts only

1 tbsp chopped coriander (cilantro)

Heat the oil in a large saucepan with a lid over a medium heat, add the onion and fry until translucent. Add the garlic and ginger and cook for 1 minute. Add the courgette (zucchini) and the red and yellow peppers and fry until the courgette is crisp-tender.

Add the cumin, chilli powder and turmeric to the vegetables, then season with salt and pepper. Cook for 1 minute until the spices are fragrant. Add the stock and cover with the lid. Bring to the boil.

Add the couscous, sultanas (golden raisins) and tomatoes, stir and cover again. Turn off the heat and allow to stand for 5 minutes until the couscous absorbs the liquid and is tender.

Once the couscous is cooked, fluff with a fork. Add the coriander (cilantro) and stir to distribute. Serve topped with Goat's Cheese, salad (green) onions and chopped coriander.

COD IN A CREAMY SAUCE
with Peas

Tender flakey cod served with peas in a creamy sauce studded with pancetta, shallots and dill will make your family hurry to the table. You can use any white fish fillets instead of cod, such as sole or sea bass.

Serves 4

oil, for oiling

2 onions, thinly sliced

4 cod fillets, or other firm white fish, 700–900 g/1½–2lb total

1 tsp garlic powder

½ tsp thyme

720 ml/1¼ pints/3 cups unsweetened mild-flavoured dairy-free milk, such as almond

For the sauce

1 tbsp olive oil

125 g/4 oz/½ cup pancetta, diced

1 tbsp Buttery Spread (*see* page 78) or olive oil

1 large shallot, peeled and thinly sliced

2 tbsp plain (all-purpose) flour or 1 tbsp cornflour (cornstarch)

120 ml/4 fl oz/½ cup chicken stock

1 tbsp grainy mustard

2 tsp dill

350 g/12 oz/2½ cups fresh or frozen peas

120 ml/4 fl oz/½ cup canned coconut milk

salt and freshly ground black pepper

very finely chopped parsley, to garnish

lemon slices, to serve

Preheat the oven to 190°C/375°F/Gas Mark 5. Oil a 2.8 litre/5 pint/3 quart baking dish.

Lay the onions on the bottom of the prepared baking dish. Lay the fish on top of the onions, then sprinkle the fish with garlic powder and thyme. Pour the milk over the top and cover with foil. Bake for 35 minutes.

Meanwhile, make the sauce. Heat the oil in a saucepan over a medium-high heat, add the pancetta and fry until crisp and brown. Remove from the pan and set aside.

Add the Buttery Spread and shallots to the pan and cook until the shallots are translucent.

Sprinkle the flour over the shallots and cook for 1 minute, whisking constantly. Add the stock, mustard and dill. Whisk well, then turn off the heat and set aside.

After the fish is cooked through, remove from the oven and carefully take it out of the pan and keep warm. Pour the liquid from the baking dish through a sieve (strainer), then whisk the liquid into the mixture in the saucepan. Cook over a medium-high heat until thickened and beginning to bubble. Stir in the peas, pancetta and coconut milk. Season with salt and pepper.

Divide the warm cod among four shallow pasta bowls, breaking up the fish. Pour the cream sauce over the fish and sprinkle with parsley, if liked. Serve with a lemon wedge.

BAKED CANNELLONI PASTA
with Spinach

This baked cannelloni is the perfect comfort food that also happens to be vegetarian. Try adding drained and chopped canned artichokes or some diced chopped roasted pepper to the filling to ramp up the flavour even more.

Serves 4-6

For the spinach ricotta filling

1 quantity dairy-free Ricotta (*see* page 67)

1 tbsp olive oil, plus extra for oiling

175 g/6 oz fresh baby spinach, chopped

1 garlic clove, peeled and very finely chopped

2 medium (large) eggs, lightly beaten

50 g/2 oz/½ cup grated dairy-free Parmesan (*see* page 73)

½ tsp ground nutmeg

For the tomato sauce

2 tbsp olive oil

1 onion, diced

840ml/1½ pints/3½ cups bottled tomato sauce (marinara sauce)

To assemble

16 cannelloni (manicotti) pasta shells

120 ml/4 fl oz/½ cup water

125–175 g/4–6 oz/1–1½ cups dairy-free Mozzarella (*see* page 68)

25 g/1 oz/¼ cup grated dairy-free Parmesan, plus extra to serve

very finely chopped parsley, to garnish

Preheat the oven to 180°C/350°F/Gas Mark 4. Oil a 2.8 litre/5 pint/3 quart baking dish.

To assemble the filling, put the Ricotta in a bowl and set aside. Heat the oil in a frying pan over a medium-heat, add the spinach and garlic and fry until the spinach wilts. Remove from the heat and stir into the Ricotta with the eggs, Parmesan and nutmeg. Mix well.

To make the tomato sauce, heat the oil in a saucepan, add the onion and fry until translucent. Pour the bottled tomato (marinara) sauce into the saucepan, bring to a simmer and cook for 10 minutes, stirring frequently.

To assemble the cannelloni, spoon or pipe the ricotta filling into the cannelloni pasta shells. Spread 120 ml/4 fl oz/¼ cup of the tomato sauce into the bottom of the prepared baking dish, then lay the filled cannelloni on top. Pour the remaining sauce over the cannelloni. Pour the water into the dish and bake for 25–30 minutes until the pasta is tender. During the last 10 minutes of baking, top the cannelloni with the Mozzarella and Parmesan. Allow to set for 10 minutes before serving, topped with extra Parmesan, if liked, and sprinkled with parsley.

BAKING & DESSERTS

NO-BAKE CHEESECAKE

If you can't find coconut cream, put three cans of the highest-fat content canned coconut milk you can find into the refrigerator overnight. When you are ready to make the cheesecake, open the cans and scoop the firm coconut cream off the top, leaving the extra liquid for another use, such as smoothies.

Serves 8–10

For the crust

oil, for oiling

225 g/8 oz dairy-free digestive biscuits (plain Graham crackers)

2 tbsp caster (superfine) sugar

3 tbsp Buttery Spread (*see* page 78) or coconut oil, melted

For the cheesecake

1 tbsp powdered gelatine

50 ml/2 fl oz/¼ cup cold water

450 g/1 lb shop-bought dairy-free cream cheese, at room temperature

150 g/5 oz/1½ cups icing (confectioners') sugar, sifted

2 tsp vanilla extract

1 vanilla pod (bean)

500 g/1 lb 2 oz/2 cups coconut cream

For the topping

200 g/7 oz/2 cups strawberries, stems removed, sliced in half

mint sprigs (optional)

Lightly oil a 20 or 23 cm/8 or 9 inch springform tin (pan). For the crust, put the biscuits (crackers) in a plastic food bag and, using a rolling pin, crush to fine crumbs.

Alternatively use a food processor. Combine the crumbs, sugar and Buttery Spread together in a bowl and mix well. Press firmly into the bottom of the prepared tin and chill for 1 hour. If you like a crispier, firmer crust you can bake in an oven preheated to 180°C/350°F/Gas Mark 4 for 10 minutes and then leave to cool.

To make the cheesecake, sprinkle the gelatine over the cold water in a small saucepan. Set it aside for 5 minutes, allowing it to soften. Once the gelatine has rehydrated (or bloomed), heat over a medium-low heat, whisking until the gelatine has dissolved. Set aside to cool.

Beat the cream cheese and icing (confectioners') sugar together in a stand mixer until well blended and very smooth, scraping down the sides of the bowl as needed. Add the vanilla extract. Split the vanilla pod (bean) open and scrape the seeds out of the pod into the bowl. Mix in.

Switch to the whisk attachment on the stand mixer and add the coconut cream. Starting on a low speed, mix in the coconut cream. When it is blended in, increase the speed to medium and blend for 1 minute, scraping down the sides of the bowl. Continue to mix, increasing the speed and beating until the mixture is becoming fluffy and holding soft peaks.

Reduce the speed to medium-low and slowly drizzle the warm gelatine into the bowl while the mixer is still running. If the gelatine has cooled too much and has started to gel, warm it slightly until it is completely liquid again. Once all the gelatine has been added, increase the speed of the mixer to high and beat until the mixture forms firm peaks.

Spoon the filling onto the cooled crust and level the surface. Cover with plastic wrap directly on top of the filling and chill for at least 1 hour, or overnight, until firm.

When ready to serve, run a thin knife around the edge of the cheesecake, then remove the outer ring of the tin. Top with strawberries and mint, if using, slice and serve.

PERFECT CUPCAKES WITH BUTTERCREAM

Tender cake topped with buttery vanilla icing (frosting), these cupcakes are melt-in-your-mouth delicious.

Serves 12

200 g/7 oz/1½ cups plain (all-purpose) flour or favourite blend

½ tbsp baking powder

¼ tsp salt

150 g/5 oz/¾ cup white vegetable fat (shortening), or half white vegetable fat and half Buttery Spread (*see* page 78)

130 g/4½ oz/⅔ cup caster (superfine) sugar

2 medium (large) eggs

½ tbsp vanilla extract

120 ml/4 fl oz/½ cup unsweetened dairy-free milk of choice, such as almond

For the buttercream

125 g/4 oz/½ cup dairy-free Buttery Spread, at room temperature

50 g/2 oz/¼ cup white vegetable fat (shortening)

300 g/11 oz/3 cups icing (confectioners') sugar, sifted

2–3 tbsp unsweetened dairy-free milk of choice

1 tsp vanilla extract

¼ tsp almond extract (optional)

To make the buttercream, mix the Buttery Spread and white vegetable fat (shortening) together for about 1 minute. Add the icing (confectioners') sugar, 2 tbsp milk, vanilla extract and almond extract, if using, and beat together until light and fluffy. If it is too thick, add more milk, 1 tsp at a time, until the icing (frosting) is the desired texture. Cover with plastic wrap until ready to use.

To make the cupcakes, preheat the oven to 180°C/350°F/Gas Mark 4. Line a muffin tin with paper cases (baking cups). Set aside.

Whisk the flour, baking powder and salt together in a bowl. Set aside.

Cream the shortening and sugar together in another bowl until fluffy. Add the eggs, one at a time, beating well between additions.

Add half the flour mixture and mix in. Mix in the vanilla extract and half the milk, scraping down the sides of the bowl as needed. Add the remaining flour and mix. Finish by adding the remaining milk, stirring until smooth and everything is well mixed in.

Divide the batter evenly between the 12 paper cases in the muffin tin and bake for 18–20 minutes until a toothpick comes out clean.

Place the muffin tin on a wire rack for 10 minutes, then remove the cupcakes to the rack and cool. Ice after the cupcakes are completely cool.

Note

Make the buttercream up to a day before baking your cupcakes. This gives the icing a chance to firm up. If your kitchen is too hot, the icing will be very soft, so chill it. After chilling, allow to soften until a spreadable texture. Re-whip if needed before spreading on the cupcakes.

PASSIONFRUIT & AVOCADO ICE POPS

A layer of passionfruit and mango plus a layer of dreamy avocado and lime equals a match made in heaven!

Serves 5–6, depending on size of ice pop moulds

For the passionfruit layer

1½–2 passionfruit

200 g/7 oz/¾ cup puréed mango

½ tbsp lime juice

1 tsp very finely chopped lime zest

100 ml/3½ fl oz/⅓ cup coconut milk
   or dairy-free yogurt

honey, to taste (optional)

For the avocado layer

120 ml/4 fl oz/½ cup water

3–4 tbsp honey, to taste

1 small ripe avocado, halved and
   pitted

1 tbsp lime juice

½ tsp very finely chopped lime zest

½ tsp vanilla extract (optional)

To make the passionfruit layer, scrape the pulp from the passionfruit into a bowl. Stir in the puréed mango, lime juice, zest and coconut milk and blend well. Taste and see if the mixture needs honey. This will depend on the sweetness of the fruit. If needed, stir in the honey until the desired level of sweetness is achieved.

Pour the mixture into the moulds, add sticks and freeze.

After the passionfruit layer has frozen, make the avocado layer. Blend the water, 3 tbsp honey, avocado flesh, lime juice, zest and vanilla extract, if using, together in a food processor or blender until smooth. Taste and see if the mixture is sweet enough. Add the remaining honey, if liked.

Pour the avocado mixture on top of the passionfruit layer and freeze until frozen through.

CHOCOLATE & AVOCADO CREAM

This is one of my family's favourite go-to desserts. So rich and decadent, no one will realize the secret ingredient is avocado.

Serves 4

125 g/4 oz dairy-free dark (semisweet) chocolate, chopped

2 large ripe avocados, peeled, pitted and flesh coarsely chopped

25 g/1 oz/¼ cup cocoa powder

100 ml/3½ fl oz/⅓ cup unsweetened dairy-free milk of choice, such as coconut, almond or cashew

2–3 tbsp agave or maple syrup, or honey

¾ tsp vanilla extract

dash salt

¼ tsp ground cinnamon (optional)

To serve

4 tbsp roasted salted pistachios

4 tbsp pomegranate seeds

Place the chopped chocolate in a heatproof bowl set over a pan of gently simmering water, making sure the base of the bowl doesn't touch the water, and melt, stirring until smooth. Remove from the heat.

Blend the avocados, melted chocolate, cocoa powder, milk, agave syrup, vanilla extract, salt and cinnamon, if using, together in a food processor or blender until very creamy and smooth. Scrape down the sides of the food processor, as needed.

Divide the chocolate and avocado cream between serving glasses. Cover and chill for at least 30 minutes. When ready to serve, sprinkle with pistachios and pomegranate seeds.

Note

To melt chocolate using the microwave, place the chocolate in a microwave-safe bowl and microwave in 20-second intervals, stirring between each, until melted.

CHOCOLATE FUDGE ICE POPS

There is nothing like the chocolate fudgy goodness in these ice pops. Better than you remember from your childhood!

Serves 6-8

400 ml/14 fl oz can full-fat coconut milk or coconut cream

200 ml/7 fl oz/¾ cup unsweetened dairy-free milk of choice, such as cashew

3 tbsp cocoa powder

225 g/8 oz dairy-free dark (semisweet) chocolate, chopped

Whisk the coconut milk, milk and cocoa powder together in a saucepan. Heat over a medium-low heat, whisking frequently. Bring to a simmer.

Remove from the heat and whisk in the chocolate. Mix until the chocolate is melted and completely blended in.

Pour the mixture into ice pop moulds, add sticks and freeze for at least 6 hours, or until completely frozen. Unmould the ice pops to serve.

RASPBERRY CHEESECAKE PARFAITS

These raspberry parfaits are not just beautiful, they are a fun, perfectly proportioned dessert. If you would like to bring these along to a picnic or other outing as a treat, layer the parfaits in canning jars and seal with the lid. Don't forget the spoons!

Serves 4-6

For the crumb layer

7 dairy-free digestive biscuits (Graham crackers without chocolate coating)

3 tbsp melted coconut oil or Buttery Spread (*see* page 78)

¼ tsp ground cinnamon

For the cheesecake layers

175 g/6 oz/1½ cups raw cashews, soaked for a minimum of 2 hours, then drained

6½ tbsp lemon juice

100 g/3½ oz/½ cup caster (superfine) sugar or 125 g/4 oz/⅓ cup honey

50 g/2 oz/¼ cup coconut oil

1 tbsp vanilla extract

To assemble

165 g/5½ oz/½ cup raspberry jam, heated slightly to make pourable

185–250 g/6½–9 oz/1½–2 cups raspberries, amount depends on the size of the berries

To make the crumb layer, break up the biscuits (crackers), then place in a food processor with the oil and cinnamon. Pulse until crumbly and the oil is evenly distributed, scraping down the sides of the food processor as needed. Set aside.

For the cheesecake layer, blend the cashews, lemon juice, sugar, oil and vanilla extract together in a high-powered blender or food processor until very smooth and creamy. If it's too thick, add a little water until you achieve the desired consistency. Cover and chill until ready to assemble.

To assemble, divide the crumb mixture between four to six juice glasses or small Kilner or Mason jars. Add a layer of cheesecake, a layer of jam and a final layer of cheesecake, smoothing each layer as added. Finally, top with fresh raspberries.

Variation

To make parfaits using dairy-free cream cheese instead of cashews, blend 125 g/4 oz room temperature shop-bought dairy-free cream cheese, 1½ tbsp lemon juice, 175 g/ 6 oz/¾ cup coconut cream and 50 g/2 oz/½ cup icing (confectioners') sugar until creamy. Cover and chill until ready to assemble.

RICH CHOCOLATE BROWNIES

To get these fudgy bites cut cleanly, freeze the cooled brownies for 20 minutes before slicing with a sharp knife. To make these gluten free, replace the plain (all-purpose) flour with your favourite gluten-free flour blend.

Serves 12–16, depending on how they are cut

6 tbsp mild-flavoured oil, plus extra for oiling

175 g/6 oz good-quality dairy-free dark (semisweet) chocolate, chopped

225 g/8 oz/1 cup packed soft brown sugar

40 g/1½ oz/⅓ cup plain (all-purpose) flour

25 g/1 oz/⅓ cup cocoa powder

¼ tsp baking powder

3 large (extra-large) eggs, beaten

Preheat the oven to 180°C/350°F/Gas Mark 4. Oil and line 23 x 23 cm/9 x 9 inch tin (pan) with baking parchment. Lightly oil the baking parchment. Set aside.

Melt the chocolate, sugar and oil together in a saucepan over a medium-low heat, stirring frequently. Transfer to a bowl and allow to cool slightly. Sift the flour, cocoa powder and baking powder into the chocolate mixture and stir well. Add the beaten eggs and stir until well blended.

Pour the batter into the prepared tin and bake for about 35 minutes. Test with a toothpick in the centre to check the brownies are cooked through. Allow to cool completely.

BLACKBERRY ICE CREAM

With just five simple ingredients, this ice cream is simple to make, and is bursting with the flavour of summer berries. Try replacing the blackberries with the same amount of strawberries or raspberries.

Makes about 600 ml/1 pint

100–130 g/3½–4½ oz/½–⅔ cup sugar, depending on how sweet the fruit is
2 tbsp tapioca flour (starch) or arrowroot powder
400 ml/14 fl oz can full-fat coconut milk
150 ml/¼ pint/⅔ cup dairy-free milk of choice, such as almond
400 g/14 oz/3 cups blackberries

Combine the sugar with the tapioca flour (starch) in a saucepan. Whisk in the coconut milk and 100 ml/3½ fl oz/⅓ cup milk. Heat over a medium heat, whisking frequently, until small bubbles appear around the edge of the pan and the mixture has thickened slightly. The sugar should be completely dissolved. Remove from the heat and allow to cool.

Put 250 g/9 oz/2 cups berries into a blender and blend with the remaining milk until smooth. Pour the mixture through a sieve (strainer) to remove the seeds. Mix the strained mixture into the coconut milk mixture.

With a potato masher, crush the remaining berries, then stir them into the coconut milk mixture. Cover and chill until cold.

When cold, freeze the mixture in an ice-cream machine according to the manufacturer's instructions, then transfer the ice cream to a freezerproof container and freeze for 2 hours to firm up.

COCONUT & LIME POUND CAKE

A moist cake with a wonderful sweet coconut flavour complemented by the brightness of lime.

Serves 8–10

oil, for oiling

200 ml/7 fl oz/¾ cup canned full-fat coconut milk

50 ml/2 fl oz/¼ cup lime juice

200 g/7 oz/1½ cups plain (all-purpose) flour or favourite blend, plus extra for dusting

1 tsp baking powder

½ tsp bicarbonate of soda (baking soda)

100 g/3½ oz/½ cup unrefined coconut oil, softened

100 g/3½ oz/½ cup caster (superfine) sugar

1 tbsp finely grated lime zest

2 medium (large) eggs, room temperature

1 tsp vanilla extract

½ tsp coconut extract (optional)

100 g/3½ oz/½ cup desiccated (unsweetened shredded) coconut (optional)

2–3 tsp finely grated lime zest, for sprinkling

For the buttercream

200–250 g/7–9 oz/2–2½ cups icing (confectioners') sugar

50 g/2 oz/¼ cup white vegetable fat (shortening), room temperature

1½ tbsp coconut milk, plus more if needed

½ tsp lime extract

Preheat the oven to 180°C/350°F/Gas Mark 4. Oil and flour a 23 cm/9 inch round cake tin (pan). Mix the coconut milk and lime juice together in a small bowl. Set aside. In another bowl, whisk the flour, baking powder and bicarbonate of soda (baking soda).

Cream the coconut oil and sugar together in a separate bowl until light and fluffy. Mix in half the flour mixture. Add half the coconut milk mixture and mix well. Add the remaining flour mixture and blend, then add the remaining coconut milk mixture.

Add the lime zest, then mix in the eggs, one at a time, mixing as each egg is added, scraping down the sides of the bowl as needed. Stir in the vanilla extract, coconut extract and desiccated (shredded) coconut, if using. Pour the batter into the prepared cake tin and bake for 40–50 minutes until a toothpick inserted near the centre of the cake comes out clean. Cool for 20 minutes before removing from the tin and finish cooling on a wire rack.

To make the buttercream, cream 100 g/3½ oz/1 cup of the icing (confectioners') sugar and the white vegetable fat (shortening) together in a bowl. Add the coconut milk and lime and blend well. Gradually whisk in the remaining icing sugar, 50 g/2 oz/½ cup at a time until it becomes a creamy, thick frosting that holds its shape. If it is becoming too thick, either don't add the remaining icing sugar or add a bit more coconut milk, 1 tsp at a time, until the right balance is achieved.

When the cake is completely cool, ice the top with the buttercream and sprinkle with lime zest.

INDEX

Entries with upper-case initials indicate recipes.

If you enjoyed this book please sign up for updates,
information and offers on further titles in this series at
www.flametreepublishing.com